Focused Instruction

An Innovative Teaching Model for All Learners

Solution Tree

GWEN DOTY

Copyright © 2008 by Solution Tree
304 West Kirkwood Avenue
Bloomington, IN 47404
(800) 733-6786 (toll free) / (812) 336-7700
FAX: (812) 336-7790
email: info@solution-tree.com
www.solution-tree.com

ISBN 978-1-934009-28-4

Teaching in Focus
A Solution Tree Series

This series by Gwen Doty, building on the success of the differentiated instruction model, offers practical advice on how to respond to the needs and learning style of every student in the classroom in an increasingly standards-driven environment. The books cover such topics as scaffolding and customizing the learning, unpacking the language of the standards, maintaining the dynamic between assessment and instruction, and nourishing in students a deep and ongoing love for thinking and learning.

Also in this series:

Words First: Learning the Language of the Standards
Focused Assessment: Enriching the Instructional Cycle
Not Just for the Test: Learning That Lasts
Creating Lifelong Learners: Nourishing the Independent Mind

The reproducible tools in this book and links to the websites mentioned can be found online at www.teachinginfocus.com.

Gwen Doty

Gwen Doty delivers seminars nationwide, emphasizing customized strategies based on student readiness. The creator of numerous accredited graduate courses for educators and the codeveloper of an online instructional database, Gwen has acquired a depth of experience in many areas—as a teacher, an administrator, and a professional development specialist. She holds an advanced degree in oral communications, and throughout her career she has trained teachers and parents in the best ways to communicate with students. Gwen has long advocated the integration of emotional and social components in academic lessons. Currently, she is an independent educational consultant. When she is not writing and speaking, she is in Chino Valley, Arizona, with her husband, raising alpacas.

Dedication

To my parents, Jean Gordon and Thomas Haddock

In gratitude for giving me a strong work ethic and the passion to make a difference.

Acknowledgments

Because each and every day I learn something new and significant about the world of education, I could never thank all those who have provided me with their wisdom and insight regarding best practices. Here I will attempt to acknowledge just a few of these people.

This book would never have been written if I had not had opportunities to visit numerous classrooms throughout the country and to observe the educational practices of many dedicated teachers and administrators. So, first and foremost, I'd like to express my admiration and gratitude to those professionals who work endlessly to improve student performance. Bravo to your commitment to education!

My colleagues and employers throughout my years as teacher, principal, and professional consultant have all had an impact on my current views regarding high-quality instructional and assessment practices. This list of advisors includes Dr. Sandra Darling, B. J. Pavlich, Cassandra Erkens, Claudia Wheatley, Dr. Jan Elsea, my mother, who was a teacher for over 30 years, and my father, who was a superintendent of schools.

Last but not least, my husband, Duane, and my editor, Ed Levy, have been ever-patient with my writing endeavors and always willing to listen and advise when I needed it. Many thanks for your support and encouragement!

Table of Contents

Introduction 1

What Is Focused Instruction? 1

How Does It Compare to Other Instructional Models? 1

Direct Instruction 2

Indirect Instruction 2

Differentiated Instruction 3

How Focused Instruction Integrates the Three Instructional Models 4

How Focused Instruction Benefits Diverse Learners 5

Chapter 1: Understanding Focused Instruction 7

Brain Activators: Working With What Students Already Know 7

Brain Activator: The Language of Focused Instruction 8

How and Why Focused Instruction Works 9

How Does It Work? 10

Why Does It Work? 15

Mrs. Javante's Third-Grade Classroom 16

Planning a Six-Day Unit 18

Thinking About Your Thinking 25

Read All About It! 25

Tools and Templates 26

Chapter 2: What Students Need to Know and How Well They Need to Know It 33

Brain Activator: What Does the Standard Expect, and How Can It Be Layered? 33

Analyzing the Standard 34

Analyzing a Three-Layered Standard 35

Analyzing a More Difficult Standard 36

Layered Learning 37

Lynn Markham's Seventh-Grade Classroom 38

Thinking About Your Thinking 41

Read All About It! 42

Tools and Templates 42

Chapter 3: Preinstructional Strategies 47

Brain Activator: How Will I Customize My Lessons? 47

Which Students Need Differentiated Instruction? 48

In What Areas Do They Need It? 50

Meeting the Needs of Diverse Learners 50

Culturally Diverse Students 50

English-Language Learners 51

Children of Poverty 52

Special Education Students 53

Gifted and High-Ability Students 54

Students With Attention Deficit Hyperactivity Disorder 54

Enrique Lopez's Sixth-Grade Class 56

Building the Customized Course of Study 60

Customizing the Content 61

Customizing the Course of Action 61

Customizing the Final Student Product 61

Customizing the Learning Using the 11-Step Process 66

Thinking About Your Thinking 77

Read All About It! 78

Tools and Templates 79

Chapter 4: The Focused Instruction Plan 91

Brain Activator: Effective Instructional Strategies 91

Choosing Specific Teaching Strategies: What Do My Students Need? 91

Creating Personalized Learning Time 93

Learning the Language of the Standard 97

Concept Attainment 99

Scaffolding the Learning 101

Customizing the Learning Groups 105

Measuring Success 113

Thinking About Your Thinking 117

Read All About It! 117

Tools and Templates 118

Chapter 5: Implementation and Reflections on Your Learning 125

Brain Activator: Putting It All Together 125

Chapters 1–4 Review 126

Complete Sample Lessons From Start to Finish 129

Focused Instruction Lesson: Elementary 129

Focused Instruction Lesson: Secondary 135

Putting It All Together: The Focused Instruction Lesson Frame 145

Final Words of Encouragement 148

Thinking About Your Thinking 149

Read All About It! 150

Tools and Templates 150

References and Resources 155

Introduction

Focused Instruction: An Innovative Teaching Model for All Learners introduces one of the most powerful instructional models available to teachers. Using this research-based design, teachers can easily differentiate learning content, course of action, and final student product, while maintaining a student-centered classroom.

What Is Focused Instruction?

Focused instruction is a well-planned, standards-based lesson map. This map includes the teaching components that are crucial for a deep, long-term understanding of individual student learning needs. Focused instruction involves sequential instruction that is purposeful, engaging, relevant, and customized for unique learners. This book organizes this teaching model into manageable chunks, providing teachers with a simple and highly effective process—one that empowers them to address their students' unique learning needs.

How Does It Compare to Other Instructional Models?

The individual components of the focused instruction model are not original, never-been-done-before innovations. When one views them separately, it is apparent that the steps of focused instruction are based on specific features of existing models that have been shown by research to be highly effective for student achievement. Focused instruction brings these best practices together in a powerful new model and provides a step-by-step guide for teachers, along with the tools they need to support diverse learners. Let's examine how focused instruction has drawn on the best practices of three earlier models: direct instruction, indirect instruction, and differentiated instruction.

Direct Instruction

Direct instruction is a teacher-directed approach that involves passive rather than active learning. Classes follow a series of lesson steps that may or may not be scripted, and there is always a clear and focused direction to the lesson plan, similar to the following (Eggen & Kauchak, 2001):

- Activation of prior knowledge
- Stating the objective
- Modeling the skill
- Student practice
- Checking for understanding
- Closure
- Independent practice

Because this model does not consistently emphasize student engagement and student interest, the personal relevance to students of the content is not always apparent. Classroom management is fairly easy with direct instruction, since there is less interaction and less kinesthetic activity than in other models.

Indirect Instruction

Indirect instruction is clearly student-centered and has a high level of student involvement. Students are encouraged to find personal relevance in their learning activities, and teachers often use a discovery or inquiry approach. The teacher strategically creates the learning environment, the students conduct the inquiry, and the teacher provides specific feedback (Martin, 1983). This approach affords students many opportunities to use higher-order thinking skills. Teachers may or may not have clear goals or learning strategies in place. Because students are actively engaged and out of their seats, classroom management may be more challenging than in other forms of instruction.

Differentiated Instruction

Differentiated instruction involves both direct and indirect instruction, taking into account the needs of each student, including background, academic level, language, and learning style. In a journal article entitled "Reconcilable Differences? Standards-Based Teaching and Differentiation," Carol Ann Tomlinson shares her views on differentiated instruction:

> What we call *differentiation* is not a recipe for teaching. It is not an instructional strategy. It is not what a teacher does when he or she has time. It is a way of thinking about teaching and learning. It is a philosophy. As such, it is based on a set of beliefs:
>
> - Students who are the same age differ in their readiness to learn, their interests, their styles of learning, their experiences, and their life circumstances.
>
> - These differences are significant enough to have a major impact on what students need to learn, the pace at which they need to learn it, and the support they need from teachers and others to learn it well.
>
> - Students will learn best when supportive adults push them slightly beyond where they can work without assistance.
>
> - Students will learn best when they can make a connection between the curriculum and their interests and life experiences.
>
> - Students will learn best when learning opportunities are natural.
>
> - Students are more effective learners when classrooms and schools create a sense of community in which students feel significant and respected.
>
> - The central job of schools is to maximize the capacity of each student.

(Tomlinson, 2000, p. 8)

Carol Ann Tomlinson's differentiated instruction model includes all of these approaches—clear goals and learning strategies, focused direction, and a sequential learning process. However, some of the other models that have been built on her work do not take each of these components into consideration.

How Focused Instruction Integrates the Three Instructional Models

Focused instruction has adopted the components from each of these three models that research has shown to be most effective and most critical for academic proficiency. The effective traits from the direct instruction model include a clear and focused direction in each lesson, with specific learning strategies in place. These are combined with effective traits from the indirect instruction model—a high level of student involvement, finding personal meaning in the learning, and activities that encourage higher-order thinking skills. From the differentiated approach, focused instruction takes into account students' individual learning needs and a willingness to use effective differentiation strategies to meet those needs. Table I-1 shows how focused instruction draws on the typical strengths of the three models.

Table I-1. Comparison of Most Prominent Attributes of Four Instruction Models

EFFECTIVE TRAITS	DIRECT INSTRUCTION	INDIRECT INSTRUCTION	DIFFERENTIATED INSTRUCTION	FOCUSED INSTRUCTION
Clear and focused direction in each lesson	✓			✓
Teacher-centered	✓			
Student-centered		✓	✓	✓
High level of student involvement		✓	✓	✓
Standards made clear to students	✓			✓
Personal relevance		✓	✓	✓
Teacher modeling	✓		✓	✓
Various practice opportunities	✓		✓	✓
Classroom management easy to monitor	✓			✓
Discovery or inquiry approach		✓	✓	✓
Takes into account the individual needs of each student			✓	✓
Can involve both direct and indirect instruction			✓	✓

How Focused Instruction Benefits Diverse Learners

Each student who walks through the classroom door has unique learning strengths and weaknesses, as well as a distinctive path for information absorption, processing, and application. Because students' backgrounds, knowledge, and vocabulary on any given topic also vary greatly, they each perceive and interpret new information in a distinct way.

That is why for each standard you teach, you must preassess students' current level of skill or knowledge. This allows you to customize the learning for the material in that particular lesson. Rather than labeling, categorizing, or classifying students, look at individual readiness levels with each new standard presented and make instructional decisions accordingly. Whenever you introduce a new standard, the groupings of students also shift according to their needs, interests, and skill level. In some groups, gifted students and special education students might be working on the same task.

Focused instruction includes modifications and customizations for the following diverse learners:

- Culturally diverse students

- English-language learners

- Children growing up in poverty

- Special education students

- Gifted and high-ability students

- Students with attention deficit hyperactivity disorder

- Regular education students

Users of focused instruction benefit from its step-by-step, solidly researched-based instructional map, which integrates some of the highest impact strategies research has to offer. Every one of its 11 steps builds toward customizing the content, course of action, and final student product to meet the needs of diverse learners. In subsequent chapters, we will explore in detail each of the 11 steps of this process:

1. Analyze the standard

2. Preinstructional strategies

3. Goals and purpose

4. Brain activators

5. Learn the language of the standard

6. Sequential and active instruction

7. Check for understanding

8. Student practice with scaffolding

9. Teacher feedback

10. Final student product

11. Student reflections

Through various tasks, graphic organizers, and chapter activities, the research-based learning tools presented here are clearly modeled for the reader. You will find many of them in reproducible form in the Tools and Templates sections at the end of every chapter and also on the Internet at www.teachinginfocus.com. We hope you will engage with these resources and become an active participant in the learning. Doing so will enable you to benefit much more fully from them. Enjoy the process!

1

Understanding Focused Instruction

The most extraordinary thing about a really good teacher is that he or she transcends accepted educational methods. Such methods are designed to help average teachers approximate the performance of good teachers.

—Margaret Mead

In this chapter . . .

- Brain Activators: Working With What Students Already Know

- How and Why Focused Instruction Works

- Mrs. Javante's Third-Grade Classroom

- Thinking About Your Thinking

- Read All About It!

- Tools and Templates

Brain Activators: Working With What Students Already Know

The brain activator step in the focused instruction map is a crucial component of every lesson we teach. In a review of how children learn from text, Alexander and Jetton (2000) conclude, "Of all the factors, none exerts more influence on what students understand and remember than the knowledge they possess" (p. 291). Each chapter of this book opens with a brain activator for the purpose of activating your own prior knowledge and experiences. Following Marzano, Pickering, & Pollock (2001), this exercise makes use of cues, questions, and advance organizers.

Brain Activator: The Language of Focused Instruction

Chapter 1 focuses on the vocabulary that will be used throughout this book. Having a shared language to start out enables you to place your attention on the process being introduced rather than on the new words you are encountering. To learn the language of focused instruction, complete the terminology advance organizer, shown in Table 1-1. First, read the definitions for each of the focused instruction terms. Next, use the middle column to record your own background experiences, knowledge, or thoughts regarding that term. In the last column, create a symbol, sketch, or other visual aid that will help you remember the term and how it relates to focused instruction. A reproducible form of this table can be found on page 27 in the Tools and Templates section at the end of this chapter.

Table 1-1. Terminology Advance Organizer

TERM	DEFINITION	MY OWN THOUGHTS AND IDEAS	MY VISUAL REMINDER
Focused Instruction	A well-planned, standards-based lesson map that respects individual learning needs and includes the essential teaching components needed for deep and long-term understanding		
Pre-instructional Strategies	Decisions prior to the lesson presentation regarding student readiness, expectations of the standard, ways to differentiate the learning, and activities that will be used		
Formative Assessment	All activities that provide information to be used as feedback for modifying teaching and learning. They should be purposeful (for example, "What are my reasons for assessing this? To what depth do my students need to understand it?") and should also be a natural process coinciding with instruction.		
Layers of Learning	Analyzing the standard prior to instruction to determine which level of understanding students are expected to achieve: essential, application, or complex thinking		
Complex Thinking	Being able to analyze one's own skills and strategies, to think about one's own thinking processes, and to make decisions using higher-order thinking skills		

Table 1–1. Terminology Advance Organizer (continued)

TERM	DEFINITION	MY OWN THOUGHTS AND IDEAS	MY VISUAL REMINDER
Instructional Scaffolding	The support a teacher provides to promote learning when concepts and skills are being introduced to students, including the terms and concepts associated with the standard, visual aids, templates and guides, and individualized instruction		
The Language of the Standard	Learning the terms and concept words used during the lesson, which enables students to be more successful in learning the new information when they know the language associated with the content		
Customizing the Course of Study	Meeting the needs of each unique learner through differentiation of the course of study, on three levels: 1. Content 2. Course of action 3. Final student product		

How and Why Focused Instruction Works

What picture do you get in your mind's eye when you hear the term *focused instruction?* One image it might evoke is that of the all-knowing teacher in the front of the classroom, very much in charge, while students sit passively in their seats. The teacher in this scenario is probably using a lecture format. For others, focused instruction may evoke the image of someone teaching from a textbook using a scripted format. Or focused instruction may bring to mind a series of steps to follow, based on state standards.

To help you get a better picture of focused instruction, envision a target hanging on a classroom wall. The teacher is launching "instructional arrows" toward this standards-based target. Carefully, she focuses her aim and then shoots. If she can't quite hit the target, she moves a little closer or refocuses her aim from a slightly different vantage point. This visual may help as you begin to wrap your mind around the concept of focused instruction.

Throughout this book, we define this term as a well-planned, standards-based lesson map that takes into account individual learning needs and includes essential teaching components for deep and long-term understanding. As you saw in Table I-1 on page 4, the focused instruction model takes the best practices of three other well-known instructional models: direct instruction, indirect instruction, and differentiated instruction. Focused instruction integrates these models and adds components that current research suggests are most effective for student achievement gains. While direct instruction sometimes lacks active student involvement and indirect instruction often misses a clear academic focus, focused instruction can be engaging, collaborative, self-directed, and relevant. In addition, focused instruction adds a differentiated learning component in order to meet the needs of each unique learner.

Envision these different phases of focused instruction being implemented in various classrooms:

- In a fourth-grade classroom, a teacher activates students' prior knowledge by showing a video clip about Native Americans.

- Fifth-grade students work as partners on a narrative writing piece.

- Ninth-graders share their writing through oral presentations.

Each of these snapshots demonstrates a component of focused instruction; but done in isolation, none of them is as effective as when done together with other components. For focused instruction to become truly valuable and have the greatest impact on student learning, all its components must be used—and in a fairly sequential order.

How Does It Work?

In the focused instruction approach, you scaffold the learning in such a way that you gradually relinquish control over the learning to the students as they become more adept at the skills being taught. During initial instruction, you present the goals and purposes, followed by an activity that activates prior student knowledge. Content instruction is active and follows a logical sequence. Throughout the lesson, you check for student understanding. During the practice step, you initially "control" the learning ("Let's all look together to find the words that need capitals"); this step is followed by coached practice and finally by independent practice. Give feedback and suggestions throughout the practice phase, and allow students to make corrections, modifications, and improvements to their work. Then assess understanding and ask students to reflect on their learning through logs, journals, discussion groups, or other methods.

Now let's take a closer look at the Map for Focused Instruction, which we glimpsed in the introduction. This sequence of lesson components, when combined with diverse learner strategies, creates a powerful recipe for student success. You will find this map in reproducible form in the Tools and Templates section at the end of the chapter as well as at www.teachinginfocus.com.

The 11-Step Map for Focused Instruction

1. Analyze the standard. The first step involves analyzing the standard to determine what it is actually asking you to teach. Teachers begin their lesson preparation by deciding what they need to teach, how much in depth they need to go, and what students are expected to know by the end of the lesson. We group standards into the following three layers:

1. Essential knowledge—The standard is calling for basic knowledge and understanding.

2. Application of new learning—The standard is asking students to use or apply their knowledge.

3. Complex thinking—The standard is asking students to analyze, make judgments about, or synthesize what they have learned.

2. Preinstructional strategies. This is a planning step prior to the actual teaching of the lesson. The teacher does the following:

• Makes determinations regarding in which "layer of learning" each student needs to begin—whether that means backing up to learn essential knowledge before proceeding to the standard's requirement or beginning at a level well past it. All students have to succeed in the layer of learning that the standard calls for, but with each new standard introduced, the teacher customizes the lessons in accordance with students' preassessment results, Student Attribute Charts, and teacher observations.

- Plans and creates the various assessments that will take place throughout the learning (that is, pretest, ongoing checks for understanding with feedback, and final demonstration of knowledge)

- Becomes aware of students' uniquenesses in addition to their academic skill levels; knowing students' cultures, language, background experiences, and interests helps teachers prepare them better for a lesson.

3. Goals and purpose. Students should be told exactly what it is that they are expected to learn and why they should learn it:

"In today's lesson, you will be learning the meaning of three different forms of government—democracy, military dictatorship, and monarchy. You'll then compare and contrast these three forms of government and take a stance regarding which you'd most like to live under. You'll need to pay attention to the plusses and minuses of each form of government so that you can write a persuasive paragraph."

4. Brain activators. Research shows that students learn and retain information better when they can associate it with something that they already know. Ways to activate prior knowledge include the following:

- Having a discussion—"Tell me what you already know about. . . ."

- Making connections—"Last week, we learned about three forms of government. This week, we'll learn about two more, aristocracy and communism, and then I'll ask you to make some judgments and personal decisions about all five of them."

- Using graphic organizers, participating in cooperative discussion groups, and journaling

5. Learn the language of the standard. Students need to know the terms and concept words that will be used during the lesson so that they can be more successful in learning the new information.

- Activate students' prior knowledge about a term or concept; or, if they have no prior knowledge, create an experience to give them that knowledge.

- Teach a word or concept definition, and then ask students to create their own definition and visual representation of the word.

- Provide multiple exposures to new terms through a variety of modalities (verbally, visually, and kinesthetically).

- Revisit student-created definitions and visual representations periodically and allow students to revise, modify, and update their definitions and visuals.

(Marzano, Pickering, & Pollock, 2001)

6. Sequential and active instruction. Research demonstrates that lecturing is the least effective way to instruct students. They must be actively engaged as they learn new content. As you teach, students need to be *doing*—taking notes, discussing the material, role-playing, drawing diagrams, getting involved in activities that get them out of their seats, and so on. This applies from kindergarteners to adult learners! Here are two examples of how to engage students kinesthetically:

- "Stand up if you agree with this statement. . . ."

- "If you think the answer is 'A,' go to this corner and discuss with others the reasons for your answer . . ."

Instruction should never be a passive experience for students. As you teach, be aware of the expectations of the standard, and create teaching activities that will differentiate on the basis of the three layers of student readiness: the essential knowledge layer, the application layer, and the complex-thinking layer. The goal is to bring all students to the level of the standard. For example, if a standard is written at the application level, some students may need to start with an essential understanding and work their way toward the standard's expectation. Other students, who have already achieved the standard expectation, may need activities to bring them to the complex-thinking level. You can determine starting points for each student after reviewing the pretest that students have completed. The standard in Table 1-2 is written at the essential level. John is ready to learn at the level of the standard, while Marcia and Enrique are learning above it.

Table 1-2. Student Readiness Compared to the Expectation of the Standard

STUDENT	STANDARD 1 EXPECTATION: ESSENTIAL LAYER
John	E (Essential level)
Marcia	A (Application level)
Enrique	C (Complex-thinking level)

7. Check for understanding. Instead of asking, "Are there any questions?" ask specific questions of your students, or engage them in summarizing the main points you have taught. For example, you could say, "Let's summarize what we have learned about five different forms of government." Other methods for checking student understanding include short journal reflections, student discussion groups, or a partner dialogue about the new learning. When students are engaged in discussion, listen to the level of understanding that they express. This step is part of the formative assessment process of continuously checking for the level of students' understanding.

8. Student practice with scaffolding. After instruction, students need an opportunity to practice what has been taught. Practice takes place through partner work, solving problems, journaling, and a variety of other means. This step is different from a final assessment, in that students are not yet expected to have mastered the concepts and will receive immediate feedback on their work. Students engage in practice through the following scaffolded levels:

1. Controlled practice—Following teacher modeling, students receive clear expectations for a task. The teacher and students work through the task together, utilizing discussion and feedback.

2. Coached practice—Following explicit instructions for task expectations, students take more responsibility for the learning but are still monitored and guided by the teacher. This phase involves cues, prompts, questions, and feedback from the teacher.

3. Independent practice—After receiving clear expectations for the learning, students work independently on the learning task. The teacher continues to

provide cues, prompts, or feedback as needed, but transfers the responsibility for learning to the students.

9. Teacher feedback. Each student needs feedback on what he or she is doing correctly or incorrectly, along with suggestions for improvement. Provide feedback in small conference groups that include yourself and several students or through written suggestions or one-on-one discussions, as students continue to work on the assignment.

10. Final student product. This is the students' opportunity to show how well they have mastered the material. The ideal assessment should show learning in a more meaningful way than a paper or pencil test. Examples of final student product include student-written stories or essays, projects, journal reflections, science experiments, oral presentations, skits, and so on. Performance assessments such as these can always be graded with a rubric. You may also choose to include selected response assessment items, such as multiple choice or true/false statements.

11. Student reflections. Students need opportunities to think about and process the learning. They can express what they have learned or share their feelings about the newly learned concepts through journaling, partner discussions, group interaction, whole class dialogue, and similar activities. Opportunities for reflection allow students to process the learning on a deeper level and to transfer newly learned concepts into long-term memory.

Why Does It Work?

Focused instruction works because it allows the teacher and the student to be clear about learning expectations. Lessons include explaining, modeling, active student involvement, opportunities for practice, feedback, and time to process new learning. As a result, students are more likely to *transfer* their learning; that is, to apply something learned at one time to another situation.

Classroom management is usually more effective with a focused instruction approach, because the learning plan is well thought out and sequentially delivered. The teacher maintains an academic focus and uses available instructional time to initiate and facilitate students' learning activities; the number of interruptive behaviors decreases; and teachers collaborate with students regarding the choice of tasks, keeping in mind each individual's content readiness and interests.

In their book *Strategies for Teachers: Teaching Content and Thinking Skills,* authors Eggen and Kauchak (2001) share researched-based findings about instructional effectiveness that have much in common with focused instruction. They found that teacher skills and strategies that influence student learning must involve the following:

- Identifying clear learning goals

- Providing examples and representations that help students acquire a deep understanding of the topics they study

- Requiring students to be actively involved in the learning process

- Guiding learners rather than lecturing them; keeping the goal in mind while students are actively engaged in learning

- Monitoring students; checking their verbal and nonverbal behaviors to determine their understanding of the learning

- Questioning students to enhance their understanding

- Teaching precise terminology; defining and explaining ideas clearly; eliminating vague terms

- Aligning goals or standards with congruent activities; ensuring that what has been taught directly pertains to the activity that students have been asked to complete

- Giving feedback to students that is immediate, specific, informative, based on performance, and positive in emotional tone

Mrs. Javante's Third-Grade Classroom

To bring to life the Map for Focused Instruction, we offer the following narrative account of a third-grade classroom. Mrs. Javante has a group of students, each of whom is unique in thinking and learning styles, behavior, culture, and background experiences. We'll set the scene for you with a typical morning in Mrs. Javante's classroom, followed by a 6-day unit that embodies the steps to focused instruction.

Mrs. Javante's Classroom

Ten minutes after class has started, Sierra stomps in, barefoot, one muddy shoe sticking out of her backpack. She loudly announces her arrival by complaining about the puddles that she had to go through on her way to school. Mrs. Javante patiently stops what she is doing to ask Sierra to join the rest of the class in their circle on the floor.

During morning circle, Juan, who understands very little English, begins to make loud clicking noises with his teeth and tongue because he is bored. Mrs. Javante asks his peer partner to translate some of the conversation that is going on in the group for him. She also asks Juan if he would like to share today.

Nathan, who is hearing impaired, is having trouble with his hearing aid. The battery seems to be failing, and Nathan is frustrated. Mrs. Javante sends him to the nurse for a new battery.

Linda is having trouble sitting still. She enjoys morning circle, and when it's her turn to share, she usually loves to tell about her adventures playing football or climbing trees or wrestling with her brother. But it's painful for her to sit still and refrain from making noises for more than a nanosecond. Mrs. Javante notices that Linda has reached her limit and hands her two squeezy balls, one for each hand.

Mrs. Javante next sees Sierra picking mud off her shoes and throwing it at other students in the circle. She reminds Sierra of the expectations for morning circle and the consequences when those expectations are not met. A few minutes later, Sierra once again throws mud at other members of the group. Mrs. Javante apologizes to the student who is speaking and asks Sierra to leave the group and begin her morning work from her desk.

Although the diverse needs of her students sometimes conflict when she brings the group together for morning circle, Mrs. Javante feels that this morning ritual is absolutely necessary for starting each day. First, Mrs. Javante wants her students to start their day on a positive note, and she gives each child a "1-minute share," a time to express something positive in their lives; occasionally, a student may prefer to pass.

Her second objective regarding this morning tradition involves setting the expectations for the day. Her students all have a personalized learning time with activities that relate to the objectives for the week. She takes this time to set the tone for the morning work and remind students that they will each have one free pass to ask a peer partner for help with their work if needed.

Before excusing students from the circle, Mrs. Javante also asks them to communicate their expectations regarding the quality of the work that will be turned in at the end of the week. She asks students to go back to their work areas to begin their personalized work, while she requests a group of five students to meet her with their work at the back table. Over the next 5 days, she will provide assistance to these five students, all of whom need support with two-step math problem-solving.

Planning a 6-Day Unit

Prior to Day One

Step 1: Analyze the standard. Mrs. Javante has read and analyzed the standards that she will be teaching:

- Identify evidence that the sun is the natural source of heat and light on earth (for example, warm surfaces, shadows, shade).
- Describe the distinguishing characteristics of the sun.

Step 2: Preinstructional strategies. Prior to the lesson, Mrs. Javante checks her Student Attribute Chart to refresh her memory regarding students with language or reading challenges, students with limited vocabularies, and students with life experiences conditioned by poverty. She brings together a small group of students prior to the lesson to preteach some of the concepts and terms that may be difficult for these learners.

Day 1

Mrs. Javante plays the "transition" music, which signals to students that they will be changing tasks. She then asks students to completely clear their desktops, except for one crayon or marker. Mrs. Javante asks a student to pass out the mind-map handout to all students. Once all students are in the ready mode, Mrs. Javante introduces her lesson.

Step 3: Goals and purpose. "Girls and boys, today we'll be learning about the earth's most necessary star, our sun." She holds up a poster of the sun with all of the components labeled. "At the end of our little unit, you will know many reasons that the sun is very important to you!" she said. "During our lessons, here is what I want you to think about—important concepts about the sun and why it is so essential to our earth and to you. Later, you'll be creating a project to demonstrate your learning."

Step 4: Brain activators. Mrs. Javante then tapes a piece of large flip-chart paper on the wall and draws a line down the middle. She says, "Let's list what we already know about our sun on this side, and on the other side we'll make a list of what more we'd like to learn." Students orally share information while Mrs. Javante writes it on the chart. This activity allows Mrs. Javante to preassess students' current understanding of the sun's attributes.

Step 5: Learn the language of the standard. Next, Mrs. Javante draws students' attention to the mind map she gave them. In the middle of the map, students write "The Sun." On the wheels going around the center circle, they begin to list the important terms Mrs. Javante wants them to become familiar with. She writes each term on the whiteboard, along with its definition. She asks some students to put the definition in their own words on their mind map. She asks other students, such as her English-language learners, to write the word and draw a picture or symbol that will help them to remember what it means. Students then share their new definitions and pictures in their groups. Mrs. Javante meets later with students who have reading and writing challenges to reinforce the understanding of new concepts.

Day 2

Step 6: Sequential and active instruction. Mrs. Javante has predetermined, based on reading data and other preassessment information, how to group her students for this lesson. She has created a checklist of expectations for students needing the essential knowledge layer of learning, those ready for the application layer of learning, and those ready for the complex-thinking layer of learning. After morning circle, while students are doing their individualized morning work, Mrs. Javante calls a group of students to the table to preteach some of the story concepts that she will be using in the upcoming lesson. Mrs. Javante knows that she must keep her diverse group of students actively involved during the instruction of the lesson.

When the lesson begins, she asks students to retrieve their mind maps from the previous day. While they do this, Mrs. Javante passes out a picture book called *The Sun* to each student. They briefly review the concepts that they learned the previous day, and then Mrs. Javante takes them through the process of previewing the book and visualizing the sun's components.

She then models the use of thinking aloud by reading the first two pages, stopping to make "I-wonder" statements, and asking questions. She asks another student to read the next page, using I-wonder statements and asking questions. Then she asks students to read the next eight pages with a partner, using I-wonder statements and asking questions.

Mrs. Javante sits with learners who are not yet proficient with reading fluency, and they work through these pages together.

Step 7: Check for understanding. Throughout the lesson, Mrs. Javante checks for understanding in a multitude of ways:

- "Stand up if you agree with this statement."

- "Let's summarize what we know at this point."

- "Use your journals to list something important that you have learned so far in this lesson."

- "Share your understanding with your partner."

Day 3

Step 8: Student practice with scaffolding—controlled practice. Mrs. Javante reviews all of the essential concepts that students have learned about the sun while students use a graphic organizer to record the important information. They are then asked to share with a partner the reasons that the sun is so important to our earth. Partner groups then create posters to demonstrate the essential concepts and the sun's importance.

Day 4

Step 8: Student practice with scaffolding—coached practice. Students have been given feedback and suggestions based on their poster assignments. They are now asked to begin planning a project to demonstrate their learning about the sun and its importance to the earth. Mrs. Javante has created a rubric guide that includes the standards for essential mastery of grade-level objectives, as well as application standards for students who need to use higher levels of skills and thinking strategies. This will allow her to meet the needs of her different learners.

The project rubric in Table 1-3 outlines the components that their projects must contain. Some of the choices include a model of the sun, a written report, an oral presentation, a detailed drawing, or a song about the sun. Mrs. Javante also provides students with a project planning sheet, shown in Figure 1-1 (pages 22–23), and coaches them as they create their plans. (Both the rubric and planning sheet can be found in reproducible form in the Tools and Templates section at the end of this chapter or at www.teachinginfocus.com.) As the students begin to plan their projects, some may decide to work in teams, and some students may need more coaching than others.

Table 1-3. Rubric for Mrs. Javante's "Sun" Project

CRITERIA	LAYER 3: COMPLEX THINKING	LAYER 2: APPLICATION	LAYER 1: ESSENTIAL KNOWLEDGE	NOVICE
Vision: Do I have a clear idea of where I am headed with this project? Can I picture the final outcome?	Has clear and insightful vision of final product—project planning sheet includes sequential planning steps, accurate information, and a detailed sketch of final product	Has a vision of final product—project planning sheet shows mostly sequential planning steps, fairly accurate information, and a sketch of final product that has few details	Has an indefinite vision of final product—project planning sheet shows vague planning steps, information that is somewhat accurate, and a sketch of final product that is lacking in details	Has little or no vision regarding final product, evidenced by a poorly executed planning sheet with little or no accuracy
Knowledge: How well can I use the terms and concepts that were taught to me?	Demonstrates thorough and introspective knowledge of all important concepts and terms related to the sun	Demonstrates sufficient knowledge of all important concepts and terms related to the sun	Demonstrates essential knowledge of most concepts and terms related to the sun	Demonstrates little or no knowledge of most concepts and terms related to the sun
Appeal: Is my project appealing to look at? Is it neatly done? Is it creative?	Exhibits uniquely creative, appealing, and visually pleasing project, neatly displayed and organized	Exhibits fairly creative, appealing, and visually pleasing project, neatly displayed and organized	Exhibits a somewhat visually pleasing project that may be lacking in creativity, neatness, or organization	Exhibits a project that is lacking in visual appeal, creativity, neatness, and organization
Presentation: How well can I explain my project and my new knowledge?	Presents project to class showing clear and thorough knowledge of standards, terms, and concepts with perceptive insights	Presents project to class showing knowledge of standards, terms, and concepts with some insights	Presents project to class demonstrating basic knowledge of standards, terms, and concepts with little insight	Presents project to class demonstrating little or no knowledge regarding content standards, terms, and concepts

Figure 1-1 shows the project plan one student created for the sun project.

Project Planning: Mrs. Javante's "Sun" Project

Student Name: ___Glenda Henry___

Project Due Date: ___May 10, 2008___

1. What terms and concepts do I already know, and what do I need to know for this project?

TERMS		CONCEPTS	
Know	**Need to Know**	**Know**	**Need to Know**
Model	Revolution	Sun	Solar eclipse
Control	Revolve	Star	Galaxy
		Energy	Magnetic field
			Solar system
			Earth's climate

2. How will I show my learning? (For example, a model of the sun, a written report, an oral presentation, a detailed drawing, or a song)

I will create a model of the sun that shows how earth revolves around the sun because of the magnetic field. I'll also make up a song that tells about how the sun's light supports almost all life on our earth and how the sun controls our climate.

3. What materials will I need to make my project?

Two balloons, paper-maché, paint, wire, and paper

Figure 1-1. Project Planning Sheet for Sun Project

4. How will I make sure that I'm showing my learning in this project?

I will keep looking at the rubric and I will make sure that I'm showing how the sun has a big impact on the earth's climate and revolution. The model will show how the earth revolves around the sun because of the magnetic field. The song will tell how the sun controls our climate and supports life on earth.

5. What will I do first, second, and third to create my project?

First, I will read information that tells me more about the magnetic field of the sun and how it affects the earth's revolution around the sun. Then I will research information that tells me more about how the sun supports all of earth's life and how the sun causes our climate. I want to give good examples of how the sun does this. Next, I will create the paper-maché sun and earth. I'll paint a magnetic field and then I'll use a wire to attach the earth near the sun so that it goes around the magnetic field. Last, I'll write a song that explains more about how the sun supports life on earth and how it causes our climate. And maybe I'd also like to predict what our climate would be like without the sun.

6. What will it look like when I'm done? Make a sketch.

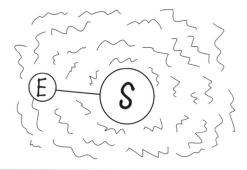

Figure 1-1. Project Planning Sheet for Sun Project (continued)

Day 5

Step 8: Student practice with scaffolding—independent practice. Students spend the next several days working on their projects in 35-minute blocks of time. They may ask Mrs. Javante for help when needed, but they are in the independent stage of practice and should need help only with process rather than content at this point.

Step 9: Teacher feedback. Mrs. Javante walks around the room providing feedback and suggestions to all students.

Day 6

Step 10: Final student product. Students share their learning by presenting their projects to classmates. Mrs. Javante uses the rubric shared with students on Day 4 to assess their proficiency.

Step 11: Student reflections. Mrs. Javante puts five flip-chart posters around the room. On each chart, she writes one of the following statement starters:

- My favorite part of the learning was . . .

- The hardest part of the learning was . . .

- What I want to always remember about the sun is . . .

- The most important thing the sun does for the earth is . . .

- What I will tell my parents about this learning project is . . .

Student groups rotate around the room to answer all the questions. Learners with language challenges have statements read to them and may make symbols for words they do not know.

This lesson example from Mrs. Javante's classroom begins to answer the questions: *What is focused instruction, how does it work, and why?* Mrs. Javante's lesson actually began prior to Day 1 when she first analyzed the standard to determine exactly what students were expected to learn and to what extent they were expected to learn it. Next, she engaged in preinstructional strategies by reviewing her Student Attribute Chart. This helped to refresh her memory regarding learning challenges that could hinder students from understanding the sun concepts. She then used strategies for creating three layers of learning that were fluid, meaning that a group of learners in a particular layer of learning, such as the essential knowledge layer, would stay together only for that particular lesson. As learning needs vary, students gain skills, or new standards are introduced, the students comprising each layer of learning may change, according to their readiness and needs.

Mrs. Javante met with one group of students prior to the actual lesson so that she could preteach the skills or concepts that she believed would be challenging for this particular group. She based the preteaching group on both her prior knowledge of these learners, which she obtained from the Student Attribute Chart, and her own observations. This resulted in these students feeling more prepared and better equipped when Day 1 of the sun unit began.

Thinking About Your Thinking

Through the Map for Focused Instruction and Mrs. Javante's third-grade unit plan, you have received an overview of the focused instruction design. The subsequent chapters of this book explain each step in clear detail and show the process for putting a lesson or unit together with this teaching model. We invite you to complete chapter one by rereading the focused instruction steps in Tool 4, on pages 31–32 in the Tools and Templates section at the end of this chapter (or at www.teachinginfocus.com), followed by formulating your current thoughts, experiences, questions, or concerns regarding each of the steps. We hope that as you read further, you will revisit this section to ensure that these concerns and questions have been answered.

Read All About It!

Links to the websites mentioned in this and all the Read All About It! sections can be found at www.teachinginfocus.com.

To gain an overview of effective teaching, read the article by Robert E. Slavin called "A Model of Effective Instruction," found at www.successforall.net/_images/pdfs/modeleffect.htm.

A number of other books and articles show the positive academic effects of focused instruction and the use of focused instruction components:

Adams, G. (1995–96). Project follow through and beyond. *Effective school practices*. Retrieved February 25, 2008, at darkwing.uoregon.edu/~adiep/ft/151toc.htm.

Eggen, P., & Kauchak, D. (2001). *Strategies for teachers: Teaching content and thinking skills.* Needham Heights, MA: Allyn and Bacon.

Gersten, R., & Keating, T. (1987). Long-term benefits from direct instruction. *Educational Leadership, 44*(6), 28–29.

Gersten, R., Keating, T., & Becker, W. C. (1988). The continued impact of the direct instruction model: Longitudinal studies of follow-through with students. *Education and Treatment of Children, 11*(4), 318–327.

Marzano, R., Pickering, D., & Pollock, J. (2001). *Classroom instruction that works.* Alexandria, VA: Association for Supervision and Curriculum Development.

The Houghton Mifflin Education Place website (www.eduplace.com) has a large variety of graphic representations. This site can be used to plan the following steps in the focused instruction sequence:

- Brain activators
- Learn the language of the standard
- Sequential and active instruction
- Check for understanding
- Student practice
- Assessment
- Student reflections

To create and print out your own rubrics for projects as well as all subject areas, visit www.teach-nology.com/web and click on **Rubrics**.

Tools and Templates

This section contains reproducible templates that teachers may photocopy and use both to master the concepts presented in this book and to prepare lessons. These tools are also available at www.teachinginfocus.com.

Tool 1: Terminology Advance Organizer

TERM	DEFINITION	MY OWN THOUGHTS AND IDEAS	MY VISUAL REMINDER
Focused Instruction	A well-planned, standards-based lesson map that respects individual learning needs and includes the essential teaching components needed for deep and long-term understanding		
Pre-Instructional Strategies	All decisions prior to the lesson presentation regarding student readiness, expectations of the standard, ways to differentiate the learning, and activities that will be used		
Formative Assessment	All activities that provide information to be used as feedback for modifying teaching and learning. They should be purposeful (for example, "What are my reasons for assessing this? To what depth do my students need to understand it?") and should also be a natural process coinciding with instruction.		
Layers of Learning	Analysis of the standard prior to instruction to determine which level of understanding students are expected to achieve: essential, application, or complex thinking		
Complex Thinking	Being able to analyze one's own skills and strategies, to think about one's own thinking processes, and to make decisions using higher-order thinking skills		
Instructional Scaffolding	The support a teacher provides to promote learning when concepts and skills are being introduced to students, including the terms and concepts associated with the standard, visual aids, templates and guides, and individualized instruction		
The Language of the Standard	Learning the terms and concept words used during the lesson, which enables students to be more successful in learning the new information when they know the language associated with the content		
Customizing the Course of Study	Meeting the needs of each unique learner through differentiation of the course of study, on three levels: 1. Content 2. Course of action 3. Final student product		

Tool 2: Project Rubric

This tool can be used for any project and any grade level. The criteria are already established. All you need to do is create the expectations for each layer of learning.

CRITERIA	LAYER 3: COMPLEX THINKING	LAYER 2: APPLICATION	LAYER 1: ESSENTIAL KNOWLEDGE	NOVICE
Vision: Do I have a clear idea of where I am headed with this project? Can I picture the final outcome?				
Knowledge: How well can I use the terms and concepts that were taught to me?				
Appeal: Is my project appealing to look at? Is it neatly done? Is it creative?				
Presentation: How well can I explain my project and my new knowledge?				

Focused Instruction • Copyright © 2008 Solution Tree
www.solution-tree.com

Tool 3: Project Planning Sheet

Project Planning: "Sun" Project

Student Name: _____

Project Due Date: _____

1. What terms and concepts do I already know, and what do I need to know for this project?

TERMS		CONCEPTS	
Know	Need to Know	Know	Need to Know

2. How will I show my learning? (For example, a model of the sun, a written report, an oral presentation, a detailed drawing, or a song)

_____

_____

_____

3. What materials will I need to make my project?

_____

_____

_____

Tool 3: Project Planning Sheet (continued)

4. How will I make sure that I'm showing my learning in this project?

_____

_____

_____

5. What will I do first, second, and third to create my project?

_____

_____

_____

6. What will it look like when I'm done? Make a sketch.

Focused Instruction • Copyright © 2008 Solution Tree
www.solution-tree.com

Tool 4: The 11-Step Focused Instruction Process

STEP NUMBER	EXPLANATION	YOUR THOUGHTS, EXPERIENCES, QUESTIONS, OR CONCERNS
1. Analyze the Standard	Teachers decide what they need to teach, the depth they need to go, and what students are expected to know.	
2. Preinstructional Strategies	Teachers determine students' uniquenesses as well as academic skill levels.	
3. Goals and Purpose	Teachers tell students exactly what they are expected to learn and why.	
4. Brain Activators	Students learn and retain information better when they associate it with something they already know.	
5. Learn the Language of the Standard	Students need to know the terms and concept words of the lesson.	
6. Sequential and Active Instruction	Students must be engaged as they learn new content. Teachers should be aware of the expectations for the standard (essential, application, or complex thinking) and create teaching activities that differentiate for student readiness.	

(continued)

Tool 4: The 11-Step Focused Instruction Process (continued)

STEP NUMBER	EXPLANATION	YOUR THOUGHTS, EXPERIENCES, QUESTIONS, OR CONCERNS
7. Check for Understanding	Instead of asking, "Are there any questions?" ask questions of your students, or engage them in summarizing the main points that you have taught.	
8. Student Practice with Scaffolding	Students engage in practice through the scaffolded levels of controlled, coached, and independent practice.	
9. Teacher Feedback	Teachers provide individual feedback to students on what they are doing correctly and incorrectly, with suggestions for improvement.	
10. Final Student Product	Students show how well they have mastered the material. The ideal assessment shows learning in a more meaningful way than a paper and pencil test.	
11. Student Reflections	When students have time to reflect, they process learning on a deeper level and transfer newly learned concepts into long-term memory.	

Focused Instruction • Copyright © 2008 Solution Tree
www.solution-tree.com

What Students Need to Know and How Well They Need to Know It

In a standards-based school system, traditional ideas about curriculum must give way to a standards-based vision. Gone are scope and sequence—replaced by a well-developed statement about how human beings learn, together with concrete examples of standards-based instruction and student work.

—American Federation of Teachers

In this chapter ...

- Brain Activator: What Does the Standard Expect, and How Can It Be Layered?
- Analyzing the Standard
- Layered Learning
- Lynn Markham's Seventh-Grade Classroom
- Thinking About Your Thinking
- Read All About It!
- Tools and Templates

Brain Activator: What Does the Standard Expect, and How Can It Be Layered?

Looking at the content standards that follow, consider various methods you might use to determine precisely what content you need to teach and to what extent or at what depth the students are expected to learn it—that is, at which layer the standard is written.

- Students will compare the settings from two different short stories.

- Students will discriminate necessary information from unnecessary information in a three-step word problem.

Analyzing the Standard

In standards-based schools, content standards guide what is taught in the classroom, particularly in core subjects like language arts, mathematics, science, and social studies; here, classroom activities should always be aligned to standards. In addition to content standards, most districts also use benchmarks or goals, which break down the content standards into more specific areas and identify the expected understandings and skills for a given content standard for different grade levels. Performance standards describe the depth and level that students need to achieve in order to meet content standards. Performance standards can easily be translated into a rubric.

Yet our students are anything but standard. All children have the ability to learn, but they learn at different rates and through different teaching approaches. In using focused instruction with diverse learners, we can differentiate our teaching and our learning activities, so that each student learns the standard through modalities that make sense to him or her. Students receive scaffolded instruction that meets the needs of diverse learners. When teachers use the steps of focused instruction in conjunction with state standards and the district curriculum, they are using components that research says are the most effective for academic proficiency.

The nationwide push for more standards-based teaching can feel antithetical to differentiated instruction, but author Carol Ann Tomlinson believes that standards-based and differentiated instruction can be compatible in today's classroom. Standards, she says, tell us what to teach, but differentiation tells us how to teach it (Tomlinson, 2000).

As we have already seen, to determine what the standards are asking you to teach, you must begin lesson preparation by analyzing the standards. That analysis tells you not only what you need to teach, but into how much depth you need to go and what students are expected to know by the end of the lesson.

Analyzing a Three-Layered Standard

Now let's take a look at several learning standards involving fables in terms of these layers.

- Students will identify the attributes of a fable (essential knowledge).

- Students will be able to summarize a fable using the identified fable attributes (application).

- Students will read a fable to evaluate author effectiveness in using identified attributes (complex thinking).

To analyze these three standards, one must look at the verbs. Less active verbs such as *know, understand,* and *identify* indicate that the standard is calling for essential knowledge or understanding. Standards that ask students to apply their knowledge—the second layer—contain verbs such as *read, determine, choose,* or *decide*—words that are more suggestive of actions on the students' part.

The third layer of learning expects students to use complex-thinking skills, which means that they are being asked to think strategically and make sound decisions based on skills and knowledge. Standards in the complex-thinking layer typically contain verbs such as *analyze, synthesize,* and *make judgments.* By getting clear about which level of learning students are expected to achieve, teachers can make good decisions about instructional practices, the amount of time needed for teaching and learning, and the ways in which they need to differentiate the content.

Essential Knowledge—Layer 1

Let's suppose that this same teacher only wants students to be able to identify the characteristics of a fable. To complete this mission, the teacher asks students to listen to three fables. Then, in groups of three or four, they complete a Venn diagram showing the common attributes of the three fables: They are all short stories, they all teach a lesson, and they all have talking animals as characters. Finally, the class comes back together to make a chart of the attributes of a fable. Mission accomplished!

Application—Layer 2

Here the teacher wants students to summarize a fable using the identified fable attributes. Now the expectations for learning are higher: They must *apply* their new learning. For example, they may *determine* that the following list comprises the main attributes of a fable: a short story, a moral message, animals with human emotions and behaviors. As they summarize the fable, students focus not only on retelling the story in their own words, but on the moral message as well as the correlation between the animal characters and human emotions and behaviors.

Complex Thinking—Layer 3

Here the teacher asks students to *read* a fable to *evaluate* author effectiveness in using identified attributes. Notice that there are actually two verbs to pay attention to: The first verb, *read,* is in the application layer, but the second verb, *analyze,* is in the complex-thinking layer. In order to analyze author effectiveness, students must first have a very strong understanding of the attributes of a fable. They also must have an understanding of what constitutes an effectively written fable that contains these attributes. Because students are being asked to make informed judgments through analysis, this layer involves complex thinking.

Analyzing a More Difficult Standard

Let's now analyze a standard that is not as easily classified.

 With a given passage, explain how the author's word choice and use of methods influence the reader and create mood.

By looking only at the first verb, *explain,* we might think this standard is calling for the application layer of learning, but let's look deeper. First, the learner must use prior knowledge to *choose* words and phrases that he or she believes will have an emotional influence on the reader. Next, the learner must *analyze* methods the author is using that may influence the reader. From there the learner must *interpret, justify,* or *make judgments* regarding *how* those words might influence the reader and what kind of mood the words might create. Because this standard asks students to move to a level that is well beyond a simple explanation, it is in the complex-thinking layer.

As you can see, analyzing a standard is not always as simple as just looking at the verb—although that is certainly a place to start. Sometimes you have to dig deeper to see the various skills or processes a student will need to use, along with those implied by the verb.

Layered Learning

In planning a lesson, then, the teacher must always determine which layer of learning is being called for. In a diverse classroom, a teacher makes modifications to the lesson plan to accommodate those students who will seek a higher level of achievement than the expectations of the standard, as well as those who are seeking essential knowledge because they are not yet ready for the higher levels. The teacher's goal is to bring all students to the level that the standard is asking for, but to bring them there in accordance with their readiness level.

In Table 2-1, we started with the actual state standard and made modifications according to the various readiness levels in the classroom. This standard is written at the application level. However, some students will need to start at the essential level before they are ready to master the standard; students who need to be more challenged for this particular standard would be given tasks on a complex-thinking level.

 Students will use the steps of division to solve a word problem.

Table 2–1. Modifying a Level 2 Standard

LAYER 1: ESSENTIAL KNOWLEDGE	LAYER 2: APPLICATION	LAYER 3: COMPLEX THINKING
Students will *know* the steps of division in a sequential order.	Students will *use* the steps of division to solve a word problem.	Students will *create* and solve their own word problem using the steps of division.

In this example, before planning the focused instruction lesson, the teacher must first have a very clear vision of what the standard is asking students to know and how well they need to know it. Analyzing the standard will 1) ensure that the teacher is teaching to the expected level of understanding, and 2) enable him or her to differentiate the learning. The teacher then decides who must be challenged beyond those expectations and who must master the essential knowledge before moving to the standard expectations. So, during the preinstructional strategies step, the teacher plans and creates three learning plans to meet the needs of students at these readiness levels.

Next, the teacher must plan how to create an awareness within students from the very beginning of the learning (whether it involves one lesson or a full unit) regarding exactly what they will be accountable for learning and demonstrating. The assessment must then reflect the goals and expectations that were communicated to students when the lesson or unit began.

Lynn Markham's Seventh-Grade Classroom

Lynn Markham teaches seventh-grade language arts and history at Meacham Middle School. She often creates units of study that integrate these two content subjects. Lynn's frustration with teaching stems from too many standards to teach and not enough time to teach them. Another source of frustration relates to having a diverse group of students whose academic abilities in content reading span several grade levels. As you can see in Table 2-2, she decided to create an integrated unit based on the American Revolution, keeping in mind the degree to which students are expected to learn each of the standards.

Table 2-2. Integrated Lesson Plan With Layered Learning Options

Pre-Instructional Strategies	Lynn knows that the history standard calls for layer 3 learning, and the language arts standard calls for layer 2 learning. She has determined which students need to begin at layer 1 before they can advance to the higher levels and which students need to be challenged to a higher degree than the standards call for. She has created variations of content and course of action (student assignments) for each of the focused instruction steps. Although her two subject areas are not completely integrated as in a unit of study, her lessons have parallel themes. Lynn will check for student understanding throughout the lesson through a variety of formative assessment formats.	
GOALS AND PURPOSE	**HISTORY**	**LANGUAGE ARTS**
Brain Activators	Students get into groups with articles they have been reading about the American Revolution. They do a share-around regarding what they know about important events and people from the American Revolution.	Students are divided into groups. Each group receives a puzzle piece from a story about the American Revolution. They determine which narrative piece they are holding (plot, setting, and so on) and must be ready to describe the characteristics of that element.
Learn the Language of the Standard	Students learn specific terms related to the American Revolution. Differentiation: Layer 1 and 2 groups will use given definitions to create symbols or drawings. The Layer 3 group will create their own definitions and drawings, with a concept map for word meanings.	Students learn specific terms related to the American Revolution. Differentiation: Layer 1 and 2 groups will use given definitions to create symbols or drawings. The Layer 3 group will create their own definitions and drawings, with a concept map for word meanings.
Sequential and Active Instruction	Lynn has determined, prior to the lesson, what layer of learning the standard is calling for and tailors her instructional activities based on her knowledge of student readiness. 1. Lynn demonstrates three different methods for analyzing cause and effect relationships: the Venn diagram, cause and effect chain, and Herringbone organizer. She has pre-taught these three organizers to some of her diverse learners prior to the lesson to provide them with background knowledge. 2. Students choose a graphic organizer, and as a whole class they brainstorm causes and effects related to student experiences. 3. They look back at their organizers and discuss specific causes and effects and what effects different causes had.	Lynn has determined, prior to the lesson, what layer of learning the standard is calling for and tailors her instructional activities based on her knowledge of student readiness. 1. When students put their puzzle pieces together, it forms a narrative story about the American Revolution. Students read the story, discussing the elements of a narrative as they read. 2. Using the whiteboard, Lynn asks students to share narrative elements and their characteristics. 3. Next, students discuss the cause and effect components that can be found in the story.
Check for Understanding	Throughout instruction, student understanding is checked through a variety of means, such as a 3-minute write, partner sharing, discussion groups, observation, and journaling.	Throughout instruction, student understanding is checked through a variety of means, such as a 3-minute write, partner sharing, discussion groups, observation, and journaling. *(continued)*

Table 2-2. Integrated Lesson Plan With Layered Learning Options (continued)

GOALS AND PURPOSE	HISTORY	LANGUAGE ARTS
Student Practice With Scaffolding	Partner teams are given an article to read called "France Allied With American Colonies." They choose a graphic organizer to analyze cause-and-effect relationships between and among individuals and/or historical events.	Students will create a personal narrative about an event in their own lives, using the elements of a narrative story. They will demonstrate cause-and-effect relationships in their writing.
Essential Knowledge Layer	**Controlled:** Lynn previews the article with the whole class using questioning and I-wonder statements. **Coached:** Partner teams in the essential layer review the article with cause-and-effect sections highlighted for them. Lynn talks with groups to ensure that they understand the task. **Independent:** Students who are ready for independent practice complete a graphic organizer with the causes and effects listed under the correct headings.	**Controlled:** Lynn provides a PowerPoint or other projection for the whole class to view that demonstrates a narrative frame. Next, students brainstorm cause-and-effect relationships that could be found in a narrative story. (Cause: A windy trip aboard a ship sailing from England to Philadelphia. Effect: A long delay in supplies reaching the colonies.) See Tool 6 on page 44 for a reproducible form of this transparency. **Coached:** Students are given a writing frame that has a section for the introduction, setting, plot, climax, and conclusion (see Tool 4 on pages 31–32). The teacher guides them to include cause-and-effect relationships in the story. English-language learners and students not proficient in writing may use a combination of words and symbols. **Independent:** Most students need more coached practice before they move to the application layer.
Application Layer	**Controlled:** Lynn previews the article with the whole class using questioning and I-wonder statements. **Coached:** Lynn walks around the room to coach groups as they look for cause-and-effect relationships. **Independent:** Partner teams complete the assignment as given but may need more guidance to analyze cause-and-effect relationships to proficiency.	**Controlled:** Lynn provides a PowerPoint or other projection that demonstrates a narrative frame. Next, students brainstorm cause-and-effect relationships that could be found in a narrative story. **Coached:** Students create a personal narrative about an event in their own lives using the elements of a narrative story. They demonstrate cause-and-effect relationships in their writing. Lynn visits this group, providing feedback and suggestions as they write the rough draft. **Independent:** Students create a personal narrative about an event in their own lives, using the elements of a narrative story. *(continued)*

Table 2-2. Integrated Lesson Plan With Layered Learning Options (continued)

GOALS AND PURPOSE	HISTORY	LANGUAGE ARTS
Complex-Thinking Layer	**Controlled:** Lynn previews the article with the whole class using questioning and I-wonder statements. **Coached:** Lynn visits this group to analyze one cause-and-effect relationship with them. **Independent:** Partner teams analyze cause-and-effect relationships between and among individuals and/or historical events using complex-thinking strategies.	**Controlled:** Lynn provides a PowerPoint or other projection that demonstrates a narrative frame. Next, students brainstorm cause-and-effect relationships that could be found in a narrative story. **Coached:** Lynn visits this group, providing feedback and suggestions as they write the rough draft. **Independent:** Students create a personal narrative about an event in their own lives, using the elements of a narrative story. They *analyze* and *make judgments* about cause and effect relationships of people and/or events in their writing.
Teacher Feedback	Students come back together as a whole group to discuss the article. Lynn puts chart paper on the wall, and as a class they analyze cause-and-effect relationships based on student practice assignments.	Students receive feedback in group editing sessions as well as oral and written feedback from the teacher.
Final Student Product	Based on a rubric, students show their ability to analyze cause and effect and create a narrative story through a student choice project. Students may choose to: · Create and act out a narrative that demonstrates cause and effect. · Write a narrative story that shows the cause-and-effect analysis of historical events. · Create a cartoon series that shows the cause-and-effect relationships between people or historical events.	Based on a rubric, students show their ability to analyze cause and effect and create a narrative story through a student choice project. Students may choose to: · Create and act out a narrative that demonstrates cause and effect. · Write a narrative story that shows the cause-and-effect analysis of historical events. · Create a cartoon series that shows the cause-and-effect relationships between people or historical events.
Student Reflections	Oral discussions Journal writing	Oral discussions Journal writing

Thinking About Your Thinking

- In reflecting on the Lynn Markham story, how might you have customized the learning in a different way?

- Do you currently use controlled, coached, and independent practice in your classroom? What new ideas or thoughts did you gain from the practice that Lynn Markham provided for her students?

- What methods did Lynn use to customize the learning with regard to content, course of action, and final student product?

Read All About It!

For articles, stories, and information about the American Revolution, visit "A Revolutionary Partnership: France Allied with American Colonies," at the Library of Congress website, www.loc.gov.

Read an excellent article by Carol Ann Tomlinson called "Reconcilable Differences? Standards-Based Teaching and Differentiation" found in *Educational Leadership*'s September 2000 issue, Volume 58, Number 1, pp. 6–11. Or search for it at www.ascd.org.

Susan M. Drake's book *Creating Standards-Based Integrated Curriculum: Aligning Curriculum, Content, Assessment, and Instruction* (2007), published by Corwin Press, offers practical suggestions to simplify curriculum alignment and integration.

For in-depth information on the standards movement and how to analyze the objectives to determine the levels of learning that are expected, read *A Taxonomy for Learning, Teaching, and Assessing*, by Lorin W. Anderson and David R. Krathwohl, (2001).

In their book *Research-Based Strategies for English Language Learners: How to Reach Goals and Meet Standards, K–8* (2006), Denise M. Rea and Sandra P. Mercuri share these proven, effective scaffolds for learning: modeling, contextualizing, thinking about thinking, and reframing information. These strategies are specific to the needs of English-language learners.

Tools and Templates

The tools and templates in the following section can also be found online at www.teachinginfocus.com.

Tool 5: Integrated Unit Plan or Lesson With Layered Learning Options

STEP OF FOCUSED INSTRUCTION	CONTENT AREA #1	CONTENT AREA #2
1. Analyze the Standard		
2. Preinstructional Strategies		
3. Goals and Purpose		
4. Brain Activators		
5. Learning the Language of the Standard		
6. Sequential and Active Instruction: · Essential knowledge layer · Application layer · Complex-thinking layer		
7. Check for Understanding		
8. Student Practice With Scaffolding · Controlled · Coached · Independent		
9. Teacher Feedback (ongoing throughout all lesson steps)		
10. Final Student Product		
11. Student Reflections		

Tool 6: Narrative Writing Frame

The following template can be used when modeling cause and effect in a narrative story.

Narrative Writing Frame

STORY INTRODUCTION	CAUSE	EFFECT
Setting		
Plot		
Climax		
Conclusion		

Focused Instruction • Copyright © 2008 Solution Tree
www.solution-tree.com

Tool 7: Which Students Need More Instruction?

List a particular standard in box 1. Then list the students who are meeting, exceeding, or falling short of the expectations of the grade-level indicator. This will help you to identify those who need further instruction.

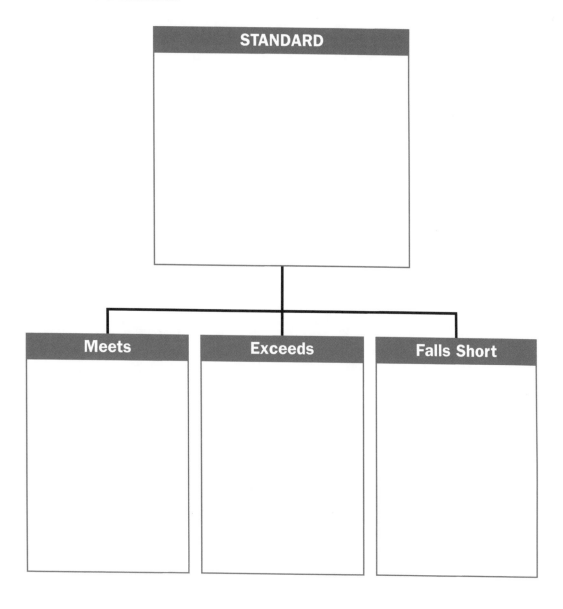

STANDARD

Meets

Exceeds

Falls Short

Preinstructional Strategies

Learning that is oriented toward developmental levels that have already been reached is ineffective from the viewpoint of a child's overall development. It does not aim for a new stage of the developmental process but rather lags behind this process. Thus, the notion of a zone of proximal development enables us to propound a new formula, namely that the only "good learning" is that which is in advance of development.

—Lev Vygotsky

In this chapter . . .

- Brain Activator: How Will I Customize My Lessons?

- Which Students Need Differentiated Instruction?

- Meeting the Needs of Diverse Learners

- Enrique Lopez's Sixth-Grade Class

- Building the Customized Course of Study

- Thinking About Your Thinking

- Read All About It!

- Tools and Templates

Brain Activator: How Will I Customize My Lessons?

Chapter 1 gave you the terminology and overview of focused instruction. You learned that focused instruction combines the highest impact components of direct instruction, indirect instruction, and differentiated instruction. Throughout the first two chapters, we discussed the need to customize or differentiate your lessons based on student readiness for a particular goal or standard. As we saw, differentiation can occur on three levels:

1. Content

2. Course of action

3. Final student product

This chapter will give specific strategies and information for customizing lessons.

Which Students Need Differentiated Instruction?

Let's start with the basics. It's important to realize that while the content in which our students are expected to become proficient remains constant, the route each student takes to reach that learning goal may vary. The students in your classroom have distinct likes and dislikes; varying academic strengths and weaknesses; and unique personalities, beliefs, values, and background knowledge. Each of them qualifies for a differentiated approach to learning. In thinking about the particular needs of individual students, it's important to think beyond the scope of special education students, culturally diverse students, and English-language learners. What are the methods that will allow *each* student to have a personalized learning plan that is also practical for the teacher?

Differentiated or customized instruction is not a program, a sequential list, or even a predetermined plan for instruction. It truly gives teachers the autonomy to be decision makers regarding which strategies will be most effective for each student. The research showing students' academic gains when teachers use these practices should motivate us all to move in this direction.

As you read in the epigraph to this chapter, developmental psychologist Lev Vygotsky (1978) discovered that students need to be taught at levels just slightly higher than their current levels of mastery, in what he called the zone of proximal development (ZPD). Mercer and Fisher (1992) relate Vygotsky's research to current differentiated instruction strategies such as *scaffolding*. Tasks requiring scaffolding, they note, are truly in the student's zone of proximal development. Tasks that can be completed without scaffolds don't lead to learning, because they are too easy. Tasks that can't be achieved even with scaffolds do not lead to learning, because they are too difficult and frustrating for students.

Effective scaffolding consists of giving students a frame and then slowly building on it until they are eventually able to complete the skill independently. Scaffolding also embodies Vygotsky's research on the ZPD in that it includes challenge, support, and meaningful feedback. Consider how layered learning corresponds with this instructional research: Regardless of the layer of learning implicit in the standard, teachers should determine in which layer each student needs to begin—whether that means backing up to learn the essential knowledge before proceeding to the standard's requirement or advancing past it.

For example, in Table 3-1, John is beginning at the required level of standard one (essential), but Marcia and Wilfredo are beginning above it. For standard two, Marcia is learning at the level of the standard while Wilfredo is below it and John is more advanced. In standard three, only Marcia is at the level of the standard. John and Wilfredo are learning at less difficult levels.

Table 3-1. Student Readiness Compared to Standard Expectations

STUDENT READINESS	STANDARD 1: E	STANDARD 2: A	STANDARD 3: C
John	E	C	A
Marcia	C	A	C
Wilfredo	A	E	E

Now consider focused instruction step 8, student practice, with its levels of controlled, coached, and independent practice—this is what scaffolding is all about. Once the teacher determines the layer of learning appropriate for each student (essential, application, or complex thinking), the lessons can be customized by building on the scaffolded frame of instruction or practice specific to each layer. Differentiated instruction is intimidating when one ponders the thought of creating 25 or 30 learning plans. But there is good news! Differentiated instruction, which is simply effective teaching that allows students to be academically successful, can be accomplished in stages. This chapter will give you some ideas to consider as you move toward a differentiated learning environment. As you read, choose the ideas that make the most sense to you, and start differentiating with them first. Gradually, just as in scaffolding students to proficiency, you can add more strategies to your repertoire.

In What Areas Do They Need It?

As you begin the school year, you will no doubt be giving pretests in various academic areas to determine your students' current level of proficiency in reading, mathematics, and writing skills. We recommend that you differentiate these three core subjects first. Secondary teachers who teach a subject area such as social studies or science will find that the strategies for differentiation found in this chapter will also be effective for them. And in getting to know your students, you will probably also be making informal observations regarding student maturity levels, personalities, verbal skills, and cultural distinctions, as well as academic strengths and weaknesses.

Meeting the Needs of Diverse Learners

Each student's learning style, strengths, and weaknesses are unique to that individual: We are all diverse learners. We also know that teachers are overloaded with the responsibilities of lesson planning, instruction, assessment, test preparation, homework to grade, reports to fill out, and parents to call. Because there are only so many hours in the day, the differentiated lessons you create to meet the needs of your students must also meet your needs as a teacher.

In this chapter, we address the following diverse learner groups:

- Culturally diverse students

- English-language learners

- Children of poverty

- Special education students

- Gifted and high-ability students

- Students with attention deficit hyperactivity disorder

Culturally Diverse Students

Students bring to the classroom their rich and varied life experiences, traditions, beliefs, and knowledge. Socially responsive teaching includes valuing each student's culture, language, and community by incorporating culture-based learning activities within the classroom. Benefits to students are increased content understanding through relevant lesson activities, shared identities, and traditions among students, and learned respect and honor for the cultural diverseness of others.

- Start by getting to know the background knowledge and experiences these students possess.

- Communicate clearly expectations about classroom procedures and routines.

- Provide feedback often, and encourage students not to give up when they feel frustrated.

- Provide relevance and purpose for the learning. Students need to know how a given concept or skill fits into their world.

- Incorporate graphic organizers into the learning prior to, during, and at the end of the lesson.

- Do preteaching of terms and concepts before the lesson when necessary.

- Follow up often to ensure student understanding of lesson content.

- Provide sequential instruction (such as focused instruction steps) to keep students focused and on task.

- Scaffold the learning so that students can learn one chunk and feel positive about their success before learning the next chunk.

- Provide opportunities for visual and kinesthetic activities during the learning.

(Burnette, 1999)

English-Language Learners

English-language learners (ELL) are students whose second language is English. These children generally have prior knowledge and experiences with language learning but are not yet proficient with the English language. Rich and consistent experiences in developing oral language are key with ELL students. Reading and writing in English are the next steps after students have become somewhat proficient with oral language. Specific strategies for English-language learners include the following:

- Emphasize the learning of vocabulary through visual modes such as creating a picture card file, making picture journals, and so on.

- Help students to sort and categorize vocabulary into groups that are relevant to them.

- Teach signal words in written materials, such as "that is," "first," "then," and "next."

- Provide collaborative partner or group-learning opportunities.

- Provide shorter or less complex activities and assignments, such as the following:

  - Shorter and less complex questions on written assignments

  - Shorter and less complex reading assignments

  - Taped short stories or other oral language resources

- Provide a multitude of pictures, charts, diagrams, graphs, videos, and other visuals during instruction.

- Allow students to create their own picture glossaries to accompany content assignments.

- Encourage students to underline key words that can later be emphasized during content assignments.

- Provide templates for students with some sections filled in for them or with visuals to provide clues.

(Hill & Flynn, 2006; Rea & Mercuri, 2006)

Children of Poverty

Students from environments where there is generational poverty sometimes feel that their teachers do not believe in them. Oral interaction, developing rapport, and becoming in tune with the culture of poverty are key in reaching students of poverty. Suggested strategies for students of poverty include the following:

- Establish positive relationships between student and teacher—this is key when teaching children of poverty.

- Provide relevant lessons—feedback must be immediate, as children from environments of poverty live for today.

- Use graphic organizers.

- Teach students to use a systematic approach to the data or text.

- Establish goal-setting and procedural self-talk.

- Teach conceptual frameworks as part of the content.

- Use a visual and kinesthetic approach.

- Use rubrics.

- Teach language structure.

- Teach students to create questions.

(Payne, 2005)

Special Education Students

Students with learning challenges come to us from a variety of backgrounds and cultures and with a variety of abilities. They have unique learning needs—needs that require intervention from the regular education teacher and often from a special-education related service as well. These services may include individualized assignments or instruction, modified materials, speech, language, or physical intervention. Specific strategies include the following:

- Break assignments into chunks of shorter tasks.

- Customize the learning to include shorter or less complex assignments rather than long written ones.

- Provide a model of the end product.

- Provide written and verbal direction with visuals, if possible.

- Scaffold the learning during instruction with the steps of controlled, coached, and finally independent practice.

- Use colored highlighters or colored transparency film to alert student attention to key points in the written directions for the assignment.

- Help students with their organization skills (for example, the use of an agenda or homework notebook, labeled file folders, and so on).

- Provide the use of a study carrel when needed.

- Seat students in areas that are free from distractions.

(Lewis & Doorlag, 2005)

Gifted and High-Ability Students

High achieving students need differentiation techniques in order to enhance, expand, and challenge their thinking in the regular classroom. Modify classroom content to encourage more in-depth thinking and research. Allow gifted students to follow a path that is of special interest to them. Also, altering the pace at which these students are expected to achieve an objective can allow for a more rigorous academic experience. Creating a flexible environment and utilizing varied instructional approaches are two more methods for customizing the learning experience for high-ability students. Specific customization strategies include the following:

- Use cluster groupings that allow high-level students to work on activities that challenge their areas of strength.

- Use learning contracts or rubrics that create a learning experience customized to challenge these students in areas of strength as well as in weaker areas.

- Implement curriculum compacting by taking the following steps:

    - Define the goals and outcomes of a particular unit or lesson.

    - Determine and document what each student has already mastered and what he or she has not mastered.

    - Provide replacement or extension strategies for material already mastered through more challenging activities, allowing for the productive use of the student's time.

- Teach students how to think from varying perspectives.

(Johnson & Kendrick, 2005)

Students With Attention Deficit Hyperactivity Disorder

Students with attention deficit hyperactivity disorder have a difficult time focusing, paying attention in class, and/or controlling their behavior for long periods of time.

Typical symptoms of this disorder may include blurting out answers, fidgeting and not being able to stay in one's seat, becoming easily distracted, and jumping from one incomplete activity to another. Strategies that are suggested for students with ADHD include the following:

- Prior to any lesson, determine with the student what the "secret cue" will be when that student needs a reminder to stay on task. The reminder might be that you discreetly place a chip on the student's desk or a hand on the shoulder, or that you make a hand signal that has been agreed upon in advance.

- Start lessons by clearly stating goals and purposes in order to get students focused.

- Activate prior knowledge (for example, use a brain activator activity).

- Use graphic organizers prior to, during, and at the end of the lesson.

- Set behavioral expectations for the lesson.

- Use structure and consistency, such as the focused instruction sequence.

- Divide student work into small chunks. An egg timer may be used for each segment of the learning to encourage students to stay on task.

- Use a multitude of visual and kinesthetic materials during the lesson, such as an overhead projector, a film clip, math manipulatives, and so on.

- After giving oral or written directions, follow up with ADHD students to check their understanding of the expectations.

- Provide specific feedback and suggestions during practice activities.

(U.S. Office of Special Education Programs: www.ed.gov/teachers)

After you feel that you have gathered substantial data from formal and informal evaluations, create a Student Attribute Chart for each of your students (see page 57). Filling out a Student Attribute Chart doesn't have to take an enormous amount of time, because after looking at all of your gathered information, your notes will be anecdotal and concise. We suggest filling out a second Student Attribute Chart in the second half of the school year, so that you can make comparisons regarding student social and academic growth.

Utilizing a Student Attribute Chart is one method for documenting the needs of each student, along with your observations and the strategies that you are implementing with each student who has special needs. Let's look at how one sixth-grade teacher, Enrique Lopez, effectively used a Student Attribute Chart.

Enrique Lopez's Sixth-Grade Class

Enrique Lopez is a third-year teacher at Miller Valley Middle School who teaches a self-contained sixth-grade class. He has heard a great deal about differentiated instruction and has even attended one workshop to learn more about it. But even with some background and prior knowledge, Enrique is still not sure where to begin the process of differentiated instruction. Another teacher in the building, Terry Jackson, has described to him how she uses a Student Attribute Chart in which anecdotal notes, concerns, special needs, and learning strengths and weaknesses can be recorded at the beginning of the semester or school year. Enrique decides that this is a good place to start and completes his first Student Attribute Chart, shown in Figure 3-1, depicting a sixth-grade student named Anthony Martinez. Enrique hopes that generating this profile will help him create strategies to support Anthony in attaining academic and social success.

Once Enrique has completed the first two columns, he goes back and fills in the teaching strategies to customize the learning for Anthony.

Student Attribute Chart

Student: _Anthony Martinez_

Date: _September 1, 2008_

SPECIAL LEARNING NEEDS	OBSERVATIONS	STRATEGIES
ELL **Culturally Diverse**	Spanish is spoken at home. Anthony speaks English but vocabulary is well below grade level.	✓ Will receive ELL services 2 times per week ✓ Peer coaching ✓ Preteaching of terms prior to lesson content

LEARNING STYLE	OBSERVATIONS	STRATEGIES
Auditory	I'm not seeing strong listening skills—perhaps due to lack of English proficiency.	✓ Peer coaching ✓ Use more visuals in my teaching.
Visual	Seems to be very artistic visually!	✓ Use more visuals in my instruction. ✓ Provide graphic organizers for him during instruction.
Kinesthetic	Athletic—loves sports	✓ Allow kinesthetic formats for demonstration of learning (projects, skits, and so on).

Figure 3-1. Student Attribute Chart for Anthony Martinez (continues on next page)

PERSONALITY STYLE	OBSERVATIONS	STRATEGIES
Attention-Seeking		
Introspective/Loner		
Social/nterpersonal	*Friendly but a little apprehensive*	
Leader	*Might demonstrate leadership skills when he gains English proficiency*	✓ *Provide opportunities for Anthony to lead during kinesthetic or visual projects.*
Peacemaker		
Aggressive	*Occasionally aggressive during P.E. and recess sports*	✓ *Observe and monitor.*
Passive		
Comments		

Figure 3-1. Student Attribute Chart for Anthony Martinez (continued from previous page)

ACADEMIC STRENGTHS AND WEAKNESSES	OBSERVATIONS	STRATEGIES
Reading skills	Comprehension—2nd grade level. Is fairly fluent in reading orally.	Preteaching of terms and concepts prior to the lesson Use controlled, coached, and independent comprehension practice with visual and kinesthetic activities. Provide background knowledge and create relevance for reading selections.
Writing Skills	Mature fine motor skills. Seems to be a fluent writer when writing in native language. May have high language arts skills when he becomes fluent in English language.	Scaffold the learning: Allow Anthony to write a combination of English and Spanish, with sketches or symbols, gradually transitioning to English.
Mathematics	On grade level with math skills based on beginning year pre-test. Enjoys all problems that don't involve reading.	Will partner him with other students for word problems.
Special Talents, Concerns, or Uniquenesses	Draws very detailed and accurate sketches—very talented in visual arts. Concerned that he gets frustrated with his lack of English proficiency.	Integrate drawing, sketching, and so on, into the content tasks and assignments.
Other Comments	Would like to help develop the leadership qualities that I'm starting to see in Anthony.	Math peer helper perhaps when problems do not involve reading?

Figure 3–1. Student Attribute Chart for Anthony Martinez (continued from previous page)

A blank, reproducible version of the Student Attribute Chart can be found on pages 80–82 in the Tools and Templates section at the end of this chapter or at www.teachinginfocus.com.

Enrique talks with Terry, the neighboring teacher who originally shared the Student Attribute Chart with him, about his first attempt. He learns that there is an additional resource he can use that will help him pinpoint effective strategies for each of his diverse learners. When filling out the Student Attribute Charts for the remainder of his students, he will now use the Instructional Needs for Diverse Learners Chart, shown in Table 3-2 (beginning on page 62), as a resource for choosing the best practices for each learner. Terry suggests that Enrique find an easily accessible location for it, such as his lesson planning book.

Terry shares with Enrique that meeting the needs of each individual does not have to be monumentally time-consuming and that most teachers who explore the concepts of "customizing the learning" find they are already providing differentiated instruction much more regularly than they realized. Based on numerous books and articles on differentiated instruction, including those of Carol Ann Tomlinson, Carolyn Chapman, and Rita King, Terry suggests some simple ways Enrique can begin to make conscious changes in his teaching:

- Begin customizing the lessons and learning activities in only one subject area (preferably reading, writing, or math).

- At first, customize lessons according to only one of these areas of approach: content, course of action, or final student product (see the following section).

- Choose just one or two of the steps of focused instruction to differentiate, rather than all 11 of them.

Building the Customized Course of Study

There are multiple methods for modifying, enriching, or adjusting any particular lesson or assignment for students.

Customizing the Content

This form of differentiation involves looking at the content standards and analyzing the learning expectations for that content. When a teacher determines that the content, or the materials to use with the content, are too difficult for some or not challenging enough for others, he or she may choose to customize it in order to meet the needs of various students. Think now about how this relates to the layers of learning. You learned how to classify standard expectations as essential, application, or complex thinking. Next, you learned how to determine in which layer each of your students needed to be instructed, and you read some samples of lesson customization for each of the layers. Armed with this information, you are now on your way to differentiating the content!

Customizing the Course of Action

Prior to the lesson, you'll want to be clear about the layer of learning in which each student needs to begin his or her learning journey. You'll need to determine how a particular student will reach the target, or objective, which may not be the same way that another student reaches it. For example, you may determine that all students will use an outline or template during instruction. Some students will have their templates partially filled in, while others will be creating their own template design. You may decide that students in the essential layer will work on a project together that you can closely monitor (coached practice), while students in the complex-thinking layer may each work independently on a different type of project. Customizing the course of action is all about how to vary the *way* that students ultimately reach the same goal or standard expectation.

Customizing the Final Student Product

The "final student product" usually equates to the last assessment for that lesson; it should not be something tacked on but should flow naturally out of the lesson. Final products can mean journal entries, presentations, essays, individual projects, or a multitude of other creations. However, along the way, you may use ungraded student products to assess their progress in mastering the content. When products are customized, the needs of individual students are taken into account. Taking a look at Student Attribute Charts, multiple intelligence strengths and weaknesses, prior test scores, and so on will help you to determine how to customize the final product.

Table 3-2. Instructional Needs for Diverse Learners Chart

KEY:
-Not an effective teaching strategy
+ Appropriate teaching strategy
++ Highly effective teaching strategy

TYPES OF INSTRUCTION	VISUALLY IMPAIRED	HEARING IMPAIRED	CULTURALLY DIVERSE
Focused Instruction With Multimodality Methods (Visual, Kinesthetic, Auditory)	++ Use large black and white print; audio methods.	++ Use visual cues and materials; clear pronunciation.	++ Use visual methods in particular.
Structure and Task Timelines	+ Provide a secure environment.	+ Provide a secure environment.	+
Preteaching Vocabulary and Concepts Prior to Lesson	+	+	++ Provide background knowledge and relevance.
Establishing Relevance and Purpose for the Learning	+	+	++ Make relevant to their backgrounds.
Learning the Language of the Standard	+ Use terms with large print, visuals, and oral info.	+ Repeat, rephrase words, use visual cues.	++ Preteach and develop vocabulary prior to content teaching.
Activating Prior Knowledge (Brain Activators)	+	+	++ Make relevant to their backgrounds.
Customized Learning Groups (Essential Knowledge, Application, and Complex-Thinking Layers)	++ Determine student readiness level.	++ Determine student readiness level.	++ Determine student readiness level.

ENGLISH-LANGUAGE LEARNERS	CHILDREN OF POVERTY	SPECIAL EDUCATION	GIFTED AND HIGH ABILITY	ADHD STUDENTS
++ Use visual methods in particular.	++ Use particularly Kinesthetic and visual methods.	++ Use multimodality methods whenever possible.	+ Less structure and more complex thinking activities may be needed.	+ Emphasize kinesthetic learning.
+ 	++ Routine and structure; provide safe environment.	++ Clear expectations, routine, and structure are key.	+	++ Clear expectations, routine, and structure are key.
++ Provide background knowledge and relevance.	++ Provide background knowledge and relevance.	++ Provide additional opportunity for learning.	–	+
++ Make relevant to their backgrounds.	++ Make relevant to their backgrounds.	+	+	+
++ Preteach and develop vocabulary prior to content teaching.	++ Preteach and develop vocabulary prior to content teaching	++ Remember, 80–90% of what is tested is related to vocabulary.	+	+
++ Make relevant to their backgrounds.	++ Make relevant to their backgrounds.	+	+	+
++ Determine student readiness level.	++ Determine student readiness level.	++ Determine student readiness level.	++ Determine student readiness level.	++ Determine student readiness level.

(continued)

Table 3–2. Instructional Needs for Diverse Learners Chart (continued)

TYPES OF INSTRUCTION	VISUALLY IMPAIRED	HEARING IMPAIRED	CULTURALLY DIVERSE
Concept Attainment	+ Provide an auditory or kinesthetic activity.	+	++ Preteach related terms.
Specific Teacher Feedback	++ Be positive, specific, and timely.	++ Be positive, specific, and timely.	++ Be positive, specific, and timely.
Graphic Representations and Other Visuals	− Use if size of print is large.	++ Provide opportunity for student success.	++ Support concept development.
Manipulatives	+ Provide another modality from which to learn.	+ Provide another modality from which to learn.	+
Scaffolding	+ Use consistent learning steps of controlled, coached, and independent.	+ Use consistent learning steps of controlled, coached, and independent.	+ Use controlled, coached, and independent lessons with visual and kinesthetic activities.
Formative Assessment	++ Allow students to often use auditory formats to demonstrate learning.	++ Allow students to often use visual formats to demonstrate learning.	++ Allow students to demonstrate their learning through many visual and kinesthetic formats.
Learning Logs, Journaling, Complex-Thinking Reflections	++ Provide feedback regarding learner's readiness, knowledge level, and interests.	++ Provide feedback regarding learner's readiness, knowledge level, and interests.	++ Provide feedback regarding learner's readiness, knowledge level, and interests.

ENGLISH-LANGUAGE LEARNERS	CHILDREN OF POVERTY	SPECIAL EDUCATION	GIFTED AND HIGH ABILITY	ADHD STUDENTS
++ Call for preteaching of related terms, if needed.	++ Call for preteaching of related terms, if needed.	++	++ Challenge to create own example.	++ Use kinesthetic examples.
++ Be positive, specific, and timely.	++ Be positive, specific, and timely.	++ Be positive, specific, and timely.	++ Be positive, specific, and timely.	++ Be positive, specific, and timely.
++ Use visuals to foster concept understanding.	++ These can help with concept development.	++ Provide greater chances for academic success.	++ Is appropriate for visual learners	++ Combine especially with kinesthetic.
+ Increase chances of concept understanding.	++ Allow students to focus on the lesson.	+ Increase chances of concept understanding.	+	++ Allow students to focus on the lesson.
+ Use controlled, coached, and independent lessons with visual and kinesthetic activities.	+ Use controlled, coached, and independent lessons with visual and kinesthetic activities.	++ Use controlled, coached, and independent learning steps especially.	+ Do not need as much scaffolding	+ Use learning steps of controlled, coached, and independent.
++ Allow students to demonstrate their learning through many visual and kinesthetic formats.	++ Allow for many assessments to be visual and/or kinesthetic in format.	++ Vary the assessment format and assess in chunks.	++ Provide rubric that will challenge learners to think critically.	++ Provide specific criteria and expectations regarding the assessment.
++ Provide feedback regarding learner's readiness, knowledge level, and interests.	++ Provide feedback regarding learner's readiness, knowledge level, and interests.	++ Provide feedback regarding learner's readiness, knowledge level, and interests.	++ Provide feedback regarding learner's readiness, knowledge level, and interests.	++ Provide feedback regarding learner's readiness, knowledge level, and interests.

An example of a customized student product might involve a research paper. The teacher might want all students to research the culture, economy, and geography of various countries. But while all students will be accountable for the same content, some final products will include more visuals and less text than others; some students will research five countries while others will research only two; some students will receive a rubric requiring more information in each category than others. This differentiation, too, can be grouped by essential, application, or complex-thinking layers.

Enrique now has enough valuable information to start the process of customizing the learning. He started by creating Student Attribute Charts that he will add to, modify, or revisit periodically as he customizes the learning for various tasks and assignments. He has posted the Instructional Needs for Diverse Learners Chart on the wall next to his desk. As he creates his customized lesson plans, he will visit this chart to determine instructional strategies that will best meet the needs of his learners. He is now aware that he can customize his lessons in three different ways—through content, course of action, or final student product. Until he is more experienced with the focused instruction approach, he will probably tackle only one customization method per lesson. As he gets more comfortable with the differentiation process, he can add more methods to his repertoire.

Customizing the Learning Using the 11-Step Process

We have already reviewed the 11-step process for focused instruction. On the following pages, for each step, we've provided ideas and suggestions for customizing the content, course of action, and final student product.

1. Analyze the Standard

Begin lesson preparation by deciding what you need to teach, how much in depth you need to go, and what you need students to know by the end of the lesson. Analyze the standard to determine the layer of learning that it is calling for: essential knowledge, application of new learning, or complex thinking.

2. Preinstructional Strategies

Determine in which layer of learning each student needs to begin—whether that means backing up to learn the essential knowledge before proceeding to the standard's require-ment, or beginning at a learning level well past the standard's requirement.

How will I customize the content? In planning for your lesson, use a uniform content that is consistent with the standard being taught. However, you may decide to decrease the content for some students (for example, require them to learn only three forms of government instead of five), or increase the content for others (ask them to combine components from the five forms of government to create a completely new form of government).

During preinstruction, you must also determine which terms and concepts will be taught prior to the content lesson.

How will I customize the course of action? Part of the preinstructional process involves determining what you expect each student to learn by the end of the lesson or unit and how you will help him or her get there.

Determine the layer of learning that the standard is calling for. Then group students into essential, application, and complex thinking groups to help with your lesson planning.

To customize the activities, look at the Student Attribute Charts to review student learning styles and academic and social strengths and weaknesses. Determine which students will need preteaching of content terms and concepts prior to the lesson. (Preteaching could occur during personalized work time.)

Review the Instructional Needs for Diverse Learners Chart on pages 62–65 to choose appropriate strategies for lesson presentation.

How will I customize the final student product? Part of the preinstructional process involves thinking about the end goals. Ask yourself, "Exactly what do I want each of my students to learn, and how will they demonstrate to me that they have learned it?" Here are three strategies for customizing the assessment:

- Use the layer of learning groups that have been determined—essential, application, and complex thinking. The final assessment can be the student product.

- Look at the Student Attribute Charts to review student learning styles and academic and social strengths and weaknesses.

- Review the Instructional Needs Chart to choose appropriate strategies for assessment planning.

3. Goals and Purpose

Tell students exactly what they are expected to learn and why they should learn it. Some students will require a variation of the content standard expectation.

How will I customize the content? When stating the content goals and purpose of the lesson, you can have three different content expectations (essential, application, and complex thinking) based on student readiness. These expectations can be delivered to students in various ways—through whole class, small group, or individualized instruction.

How will I customize the course of action? If the goals have been decreased or increased to accommodate diverse learners, provide each group of learners (essential, application, and complex thinking) with a written checklist or rubric containing the requirements for that group and that lesson. When the content or course of action is individualized, it's always best to address students individually (or with a written expectation list) rather than announce the different expectation levels for the whole class to hear.

How will I customize the final student product? There is no final student product in the goals and purpose step.

4. Brain Activators

This step reaps two important benefits. First, as research shows, students learn and retain information more proficiently when they can associate it with something that they already know. Second, formative assessment is already under way when you retrieve information about student current levels of understanding regarding the new content. As students are sharing their prior experiences and understandings, evaluate the extent of their current knowledge. This enables you to create appropriate learning layers.

Ways to activate prior knowledge include the following:

- Start a discussion—"Tell me what you already know about. . . ."

- Make connections—"Last week, we learned about aristocracy and communist forms of government. This week, we'll learn about three more forms of government and ask you to make some judgments and personal decisions about all five of them."

You can also activate prior knowledge with graphic organizers, cooperative discussion groups, journaling, and in many other ways.

How will I customize the content? In most cases, you would not need to customize the content for this step. For example, if students were placed into groups to discuss what they already know about the five forms of government and some students were only required to know about three forms of government, those students would still benefit from hearing the discussion about all five.

How will I customize the course of action? There should be no need to customize the course of action for brain activators. However, if you have given students differentiated expectations for the learning, make sure that the type of brain activator used will benefit all students.

We know that many children of poverty, English-language learners, and culturally diverse students tend to thrive with visual and kinesthetic activities. The use of graphic representations and movement during brain activators would benefit these learners. See the Instructional Needs Chart on pages 62–65.

How will I customize the student product? There is no final product in the brain activators step.

5. Learn the Language of the Standard

Students need to know the terms and concept words that will be used during the lesson so that they can be more successful in learning the new information. Vocabulary and concept instruction are two of the most powerful strategies for promoting student academic success.

We know that rote memorization of words and definitions is the least effective vocabulary instruction method, resulting in little long-term effect (Kameenui, Dixon, & Carine, 1987; Baker, Simmons, & Kameenui, 1995).

In a study of 61 learning-disabled junior high school students, semantic mapping and semantic feature analysis were found to have greater short-term and long-term effectiveness for reading comprehension and vocabulary learning than instruction in definitions. In a synthesis of the research, Daneman (1991, pp. 524–25), stated that "vocabulary knowledge is one of the best single predictors of reading comprehension."

Here are some quick tips for teaching vocabulary effectively:

- Activate student prior knowledge about a term or concept, or if they have no prior knowledge, create an experience to give them that knowledge.

- Explicitly teach a word or concept definition, and then ask students to create their own definition and visual representation of the word.

- Provide multiple exposures to new terms through a variety of modalities (for example, verbally, visually, and kinesthetically).

- Revisit definitions and visual representations created by students periodically and allow them to revise, modify, and update them.

How will I customize the content? Some students may have fewer terms, and some may have more challenging terms to learn.

How will I customize the course of action?

- Give some students more time than others to process the new learning of the language of the standards (terms and concepts).

- Use auditory, visual, and kinesthetic activities depending upon student learning styles.

- Review the quick tips listed above.

- Prior to the actual lesson, preteach terms and concepts to some students, such as English-language learners, children of poverty, SPED students, and culturally diverse students. You may choose to work with these students in small groups during personalized work time. When you teach the actual lesson and introduce the terms and concepts of the standards, this will provide multiple exposures to those who had the preteaching opportunity.

How will I customize the final student product? There is no final product in the language of the standard step. However, if students create their own definitions and visuals, they could be posted in the classroom or kept in student journals.

6. Sequential and Active Instruction

Students must be actively engaged as they learn new content. As you are teaching, students need to be *doing*—participating in collaborative discussions, role-playing, drawing diagrams, taking notes, or taking part in activities that get them out of their seats. Instruction should never be a passive experience for students.

How will I customize the content? First, determine what layer of learning is expected in the content standard. Then create varying content expectations based on student readiness, bearing in mind that all students should eventually meet or exceed the layer of learning that the standard calls for—essential, application, or complex thinking.

How will I customize the course of action? Based on prior assessments, the Student Attribute Chart, your observations, and other information, determine how to group students for the particular standard that is being taught. Since student strengths and weaknesses vary from one standard or subject to the next, instructional groups should vary with each new standard or objective the teacher presents.

Use scaffolding—take students step by step, building and expanding their knowledge base throughout the lesson.

During instruction, use auditory components, such as small-group or whole-class discussion; visual components like graphic organizers, film clips, PowerPoint presentations, and overhead transparencies; and kinesthetic components, such as human number lines, opinion corners, and answers held up on individual whiteboards.

How will I customize the student product? During sequential and active instruction, students may have tangible work results, such as a completed graphic organizer, a journal entry, a note template, and so on; but these are part of the instruction and learning process and certainly not a product to be scored or graded.

7. Check for Understanding

This step involves engaging students in summarizing, restating, making judgments about, or reflecting on the main points that have been taught. This can be as simple as asking students to summarize the learning while another student writes the points on the whiteboard. Or it could involve a share-around circle in which students tell one thing they learned that they want to remember. Or it might take the form of an oral discussion that the teacher observes to determine how well students understood the learning. There are numerous methods for understanding, the only rule being that the student must make an overt response. Asking "Are there any questions?" is not an effective method for checking student understanding, as this question does not elicit any action or thinking on the part of the learner.

How will I customize the content? When asking questions orally to check student understanding, use the layers of learning to determine the type of question you will ask a given student. For example, let's say that the objective or standard involves gaining an understanding of the characteristics of Somalian culture. If Linda is in the essential layer for this particular standard, then a question to Linda might be, "What is the main diet of the Somalian people?" If Tony had moved into the complex-thinking layer, he might be asked, "What cultural characteristic from the Somalian culture do you think most resembles a characteristic in our own country?"

This same type of differentiation can easily be done for journaling or collaborative group discussions.

How will I customize the course of action?

- Collaborative groups
- Journaling
- Summarizing
- Questioning
- Individual whiteboards
- Whole-class discussion with teacher observation

How will I customize the final student product? There is no final product in the check for understanding step.

8. Student Practice With Scaffolding

After instruction, students need an opportunity to practice what has been taught. Practice can take place through partner work, problem-solving, a writing journal, and so on. This step is different from the final assessment, in that students are not expected to have mastered the concepts yet and will receive immediate feedback on their work. These are the scaffolded steps of student practice:

1. Controlled practice

2. Coached practice

3. Independent practice

How will I customize the content? Keep the layers of learning in mind and differentiate the content accordingly. Remember that all students should eventually meet or exceed the layer of learning that the standard calls for.

How will I customize the course of action?

Controlled practice. Whether students are working on the essential, application, or complex-thinking layer of knowledge, begin by modeling and by directly guiding students.

Coached practice. Next, allow students to work on the assignment with coaching, suggestions, and feedback.

Independent practice. Finally, during independent practice, students work with little guidance or feedback. Once the assignment or activity is finished, provide feedback and determine if the student is ready for assessment.

Group students according to the layer of learning in which they are working during the practice assignment, so that they can work cooperatively. This helps you monitor, give feedback, and provide guidance to each group of students.

The whole class can constitute one group during controlled practice and can be divided into small groups or partners during coached practice.

How will I customize the student product? Students will have "practice products" at the completion of their practice assignment. Their products will be based on the differentiated content and differentiated course of action that you have determined are appropriate for each student.

In most cases, you will not grade the practice product but use it instead to determine specific areas of strength and weakness of which both you and the student should be aware; the practice product helps define what further instruction and practice you will give. If the practice serves as a rough draft, then students should use feedback, suggestions, and so on to create a final draft that can serve as the final student product.

9. Teacher Feedback

Each student needs feedback on what he or she is doing correctly and incorrectly, along with suggestions for improvement. Provide feedback in small conference groups that include yourself and several students or through written suggestions or one-on-one discussions as students are working on the assignment. Feedback should be ongoing throughout the instruction process—from the brain activation step through the end of the assessment step.

How will I customize the content? Teacher feedback should be specific to the three different content expectations (essential, application, and complex thinking), based on student readiness.

How will I customize the course of action? Provide explicit written or oral feedback to students in the essential and application layers of learning, such as the following: "I am noticing that in many of your division practice problems you are forgetting the step 'bring down.' Let's go through a problem together to help you remember all the steps."

Provide critical-thinking questions to guide and give feedback to students in the complex-thinking layer. "Can you think of another way to get the same quotient?"

How will I customize the final student product? There is no final student product in the teacher-feedback step.

10. Final Student Product

This is the students' final opportunity to show you how well they have mastered the material. The ideal assessment should show learning in a more meaningful way than a paper and pencil test. The final student product often includes performance-type formats such as student-written stories or essays, projects, journal reflections, science experiments, oral presentations, skits, and so on. The final demonstration could also include multiple choice, fill-in the-blank, or true/false items. It is important to keep in mind that this final student product is the last component of the ongoing assessment that has taken place throughout the learning cycle.

How will I customize the content? Content assessment items should be specific to the three different content expectations (essential, application, and complex thinking) based on student readiness.

How will I customize the course of action? Assessment provides information about student learning throughout the instructional process. This ongoing assessment of student progress guides such instructional decisions as whether or not a student needs further instruction or more practice. All of the previous steps in the instructional and learning process, from preinstructional strategies through teacher feedback, help to shape an understanding of the student's skill level. You may assign the same assessment format (for example, an oral report, essay, journal entry, poster, or diorama) to all students, but each of the three layers of learning should have its own rubric based on content expectations.

Or, you may allow students to choose their own final assessment format. If so, provide a specific planning sheet with a timeline, and require them to revisit the learning rubric to ensure that they are demonstrating the required knowledge expectations.

How will I customize the final student product? At the beginning of any lesson or unit, give each student a checklist or rubric regarding what he or she is expected to know and be able to do by the end of the lesson or unit. If the student's rubric contains expectations in the essential layer of learning, when the state standard is asking for the application layer, the student must be reassessed after further teaching has occurred.

Keep in mind that you do not always have to create a new or separate assessment from the assignment. The final draft of what started as a practice assignment may be used as the final product. For this to be effective, you should have provided students with coaching, feedback, and an opportunity to improve upon their first attempt.

We suggest that along with your performance assessments, you include a small sampling of multiple-choice, fill-in-the-blank, and true/false questions. There are two advantages to including formats such as these. First, selected-response formats are easier and faster to score. Second, students need to have practice and feedback in using this format to ready them for standardized tests that require it.

11. Student Reflections

Students need opportunities to think about and process the learning. Asking students to express what they have learned or to share their feelings about a newly learned concept can happen through journaling, partner discussions, group interaction, whole-class dialogue, and so on. When students have opportunities for reflection, they are better able to process the learning on a deeper level.

How will I customize the content? The expectations for content reflections will be specific to the three different content expectations (essential, application, and complex thinking), based on student readiness.

How will I customize the course of action? Allow diverse learners to express their learning in ways that are meaningful and comfortable for them.

- Children of poverty, English-language learners, and culturally diverse students may choose to express themselves through a visual mode such as a concept map that shows what they have learned, or a poster that demonstrates how they feel about the new learning.

- Students with visual challenges may prefer to participate in a lively discussion about their new learning and understandings.

- Hearing-challenged students may prefer a journal entry to share their thinking about their new knowledge.

- Special education students, when given opportunities to understand their own uniquenesses, will be motivated to discover their own best way to share their new learning.

- Students with attention deficit hyperactivity disorder will most likely choose a kinesthetic activity to show their new learning, such as a skit, project, or performance.

Sometimes reflections are as easy as a whole-class discussion or a circle share.

Use the Instructional Needs for Diverse Learners Chart on pages 62–65 to review the needs of your various learners.

How will I customize the student product? This reflection piece is not intended to be a scored or graded product, but rather a tool to gauge the teacher's effectiveness in presenting the unit or lesson, to determine the depth of student understanding, and to foster the transfer of learning to long-term memory.

Thinking About Your Thinking

The Map for Focused Instruction that you have just studied is really the heart and soul of effective teaching that customizes the learning for students. The customized Map for Focused Instruction epitomizes the integration of best teaching practices with a differentiated approach for each individual. Because we are responsible for each student's academic proficiency, we must in some way customize the learning for all. Once again, this does not mean that each student is on an individualized plan for every subject and every goal; rather, it means that the teacher is clear about where each student is in terms of readiness and proficiency with each new topic or standard as it is currently being studied. The tools presented in this chapter, such as the Student Attribute Chart, the Instructional Needs for Diverse Learners Chart, and the customized Map for Focused Instruction, along with strategies that are highly effective in promoting academic gains, are the basic resources for determining student needs.

You will have an opportunity to reflect in depth on your new learning when you use the Semantic Feature Analysis, found on page 83 in the Tools and Templates section at the end of this chapter. When you are ready to create your own customized lessons using the focused instruction steps, use the reproducible in Tool 10 to help you plan, or go to www.teachinginfocus.com.

As you reflect on chapter 3, follow the arrows in Figure 3-2 and imagine your classroom full of students. What new learning did you gain that could help you organize your thinking and create a plan that would answer these four questions?

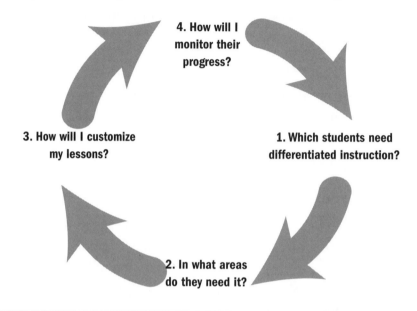

Figure 3-2. Formative assessment provides information for continually evaluating student readiness and customizing lessons.

Read All About It!

In thinking about how to best help English-language learners, children of poverty, and culturally diverse students, visit ogden.basic-english.org for Ogden's Basic English Word List. The list includes common words in the categories of operations (for example, *come, get, keep, let*); things (400 general words, such as *hope, authority, minute, play,* and 200 concrete words, such as *rug, tree, book, dog*); and qualities (for example, *sticky, stiff, straight, strong, sudden, sweet, tall, thick*).

Two very good learning-style websites are www.learning-styles-online.com and www.oswego.edu/plsi.

The following sites are an excellent way to learn more about differentiated instruction:

- www.gatesfoundation.org

- www.cise.missouri.edu

- www.teachnet.org

- faculty.randolphcollege.edu/mentor_grant/Differentiated/ differentiated_instruction.htm

Links to these and other websites can be found at www.teachinginfocus.com.

A number of excellent books contain information about differentiated instruction:

Baker, S. K., Simmons, D. C., & Kameenui, E. J. (1995). *Characteristics of students with diverse learning and curricular needs.* Eugene, OR: National Center to Improve the Tools of Educators, University of Oregon.

Tomlinson, C. (1995). *How to differentiate instruction in mixed-ability classrooms.* Alexandria, VA: Association for Supervision and Curriculum Development.

Tomlinson, C. ,& McTighe, J. (2006). *Integrating differentiated instruction and under-standing by design.* Alexandria, VA: Association for Supervision and Curriculum Development.

Tomlinson, C. (1999). *The differentiated classroom: Responding to the needs of all learners.* Alexandria, VA: Association for Supervision and Curriculum Development.

Tools and Templates

The tools and templates in the following section can also be found online at www.teachinginfocus.com.

Tool 8: Student Attribute Chart

At the beginning of the semester or school year, fill out this Student Attribute Chart using the Map for Focused Instruction on pages 85–90 as a resource.

Student: _____

Date: _____

SPECIAL LEARNING NEEDS	OBSERVATIONS	STRATEGIES
LEARNING STYLE	OBSERVATIONS	STRATEGIES
Auditory		
Visual		
Kinesthetic		

Focused Instruction • Copyright © 2008 Solution Tree
www.solution-tree.com

Tool 8: Student Attribute Chart (continued)

PERSONALITY STYLE	OBSERVATIONS	STRATEGIES
Attention-Seeking		
Introspective/Loner		
Social/Interpersonal		
Leader		
Peacemaker		
Aggressive		
Passive		

Tool 8: Student Attribute Chart (continued)

ACADEMIC STRENGTHS AND WEAKNESSES	OBSERVATIONS	STRATEGIES
Reading Skills		
Writing Skills		
Mathematics		
Special Talents, Concerns, or Uniquenesses		

Other Comments:

Tool 9: Semantic Feature Analysis

To review the focused instruction steps, fill in the boxes below with a "+" if the concept is associated with the attribute and a "-" if the concept is not associated with the attribute. You may find that some concepts require both a "+" and a "-."

SEMANTIC FEATURE ANALYSIS				
	Steps of the Lesson Where Student Attribute Chart Would Be Helpful	Steps of the Lesson Where Knowing the Layers of Learning Would Be Helpful	Steps of the Lesson Where Feedback Should Be Provided for Students	Steps of the Lesson Where the Instructional Needs Chart Would Be Most Helpful
1. Analyze the Standard				
2. Preinstructional Strategies				
3. Goals and Purpose				
4. Brain Activators				
5. Learn the Language of the Standard				

(continued)

Tool 9: Semantic Feature Analysis (continued)

SEMANTIC FEATURE ANALYSIS				
↓	Steps of the Lesson Where Student Attribute Chart Would Be Helpful	Steps of the Lesson Where Knowing the Layers of Learning Would Be Helpful	Steps of the Lesson Where Feedback Should Be Provided for Students	Steps of the Lesson Where the Instructional Needs Chart Would Be Most Helpful
6. Sequential and Active Instruction (Essential Knowledge, Application, or Complex Thinking)				
7. Check for Understanding				
8. Student Practice With Scaffolding (Controlled, Coached and Independent)				
9. Teacher feedback				
10. Final Student Product				
11. Student Reflections				

Focused Instruction • Copyright © 2008 Solution Tree
www.solution-tree.com

Tool 10: A Practice Page for Customization

Look back at Anthony's attribute chart on pages 57–59. Based on his readiness levels in reading, writing, and math, as well as his learning style, interests, and special talents, create a focused instruction lesson for the following standard:

Student will select the grade-level-appropriate operation to solve word problems.

The Customized Map for Focused Instruction

1. Analyze the Standard

What are the standards asking you to teach, and to what depth must you teach it? How will you customize the standard to create an essential, application, and complex-thinking standard?

2. Preinstructional Strategies

Teachers make determinations regarding in which "layer of learning" each student needs to begin—whether that means backing up to learn the essential knowledge before proceeding to the standard's requirement, or beginning at a learning level well past the standard's requirement.

How will I customize the content?

How will I customize the course of action?

How will I customize the final student product?

3. **Goals and Purpose**

Students should be told exactly what it is that they are expected to learn and why they should learn it. Some students will have a variation of the content standard expectation.

How will I customize the content?

How will I customize the course of action?

4. **Brain Activators**

Research shows that students learn and retain information more proficiently when they can associate it with something that they already know.

How will I customize the content?

How will I customize the course of action?

Focused Instruction • Copyright © 2008 Solution Tree
www.solution-tree.com

5. Learn the Language of the Standard

Some "quick tips" for teaching vocabulary effectively include the following:

- Activate student prior knowledge about a term or concept, or if they have no prior knowledge, create an experience to give them that knowledge.
- Explicitly teach a word or concept definition, and then ask students to create their own definition and visual representation of the word.
- Provide multiple exposures to new terms through a variety of modalities (for example, verbally, visually, and kinesthetically).
- Revisit student-created definitions and visual representations periodically, and allow them to revise, modify, and update their definitions and visuals.

How will I customize the content?

How will I customize the course of action?

6. Sequential and Active instruction

Students must be actively engaged as they learn new content.

How will I customize the content?

First, determine what layer of learning is expected in the content standard. Then create varying content expectations based on student readiness, keeping in mind that all students should eventually meet or exceed the layer of learning that the standard calls for: essential, application, or complex thinking.

How will I customize the course of action?

How will I customize the student product?

7. **Check for Understanding**

This step involves engaging students in summarizing, restating, making judgments about, or reflecting on the main points that have been taught.

How will I customize the content?

How will I customize the course of action?

8. **Student Practice With Scaffolding**

After instruction, students need to have the opportunity to practice what you have taught—practice could take place through working with a partner, problem-solving, writing in a journal, and so on.

Controlled practice:

Coached practice:

Independent practice:

How will I customize the content?

Focused Instruction • Copyright © 2008 Solution Tree
www.solution-tree.com

8. Student Practice With Scaffolding (continued)

How will I customize the course of action?

Controlled practice:

Coached practice:

Independent practice:

How will I customize the student product?

9. Teacher Feedback

Each student needs feedback on what he or she is doing correctly and incorrectly, along with suggestions for improvement.

How will I customize the content?

How will I customize the course of action?

10. Final Student Product

This is the students' opportunity to show you how well they have mastered the material.

How will I customize the content?

How will I customize the course of action?

How will I customize the final student product?

11. Student Reflections

Students need to be given opportunities to think about and process the learning.

How will I customize the content?

How will I customize the course of action?

How will I customize the final student product?

The Focused Instruction Plan

If we elect to teach a standards-based curriculum, differentiation simply suggests ways in which we can make that curriculum work best for varied learners. In other words, differentiation can show us how to teach the same standard to a range of learners by employing a variety of teaching and learning modes.

— Carol Ann Tomlinson

In this chapter . . .

- Brain Activator: Effective Instructional Strategies

- Choosing Specific Teaching Strategies: What Do My Students Need?

- Measuring Success

- Thinking About Your Thinking

- Read All About It!

- Tools and Templates

Brain Activator: Effective Instructional Strategies

Directions: Reflect upon what you currently know about each teaching strategy shown below and how you currently use it.

Choosing Specific Teaching Strategies: What Do My Students Need?

How do you know which teaching strategies to use in a focused instruction lesson, and how will you know if your lesson was successful? If you forget everything else that you read in this book, please remember this: *Teachers are the most important influence on student learning!* Teachers who are effective enhance learning to a much

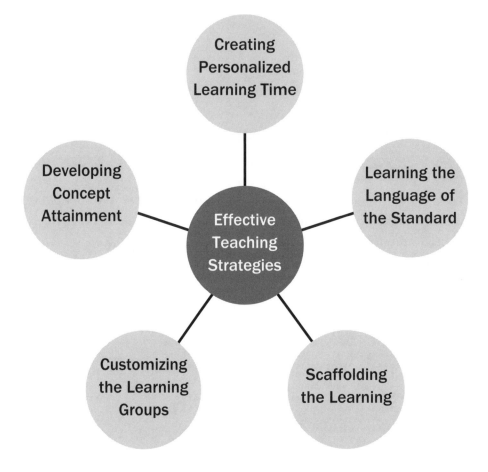

Figure 4-1. Teaching Strategies

greater level than do those who are less effective with their teaching skills (Eggen & Kauchak, 2001). Let's explore some specific teaching strategies that utilize focused instruction. They are:

- Creating personalized learning time
- Learning the language of the standard
- Scaffolding the learning
- Customizing the learning groups
- Developing concept attainment

Creating Personalized Learning Time

Personalized learning time is a short segment in the day that consists of two components:

1. Each student receives a list of activities at the beginning of the week that he or she will work on independently. These activities should reinforce the skills and standards that are being taught, and they need to be structured for the learning layer in which students are currently grouped.

2. In addition to giving students time to work on their individualized task lists, call together groups that have common needs. For example, assemble all math students who are currently working on a standard in the complex-thinking layer. This would give you time to challenge the group with complex questions and specific feedback. Or you may call together English-language learners and SPED students who need the preteaching of concepts and terms for an upcoming lesson. In the elementary grades, personalized learning may occur in the first half hour or last half hour of the day. Secondary teachers would probably create their personalized learning time at the beginning or end of a period, in a 10–15 minute slot during which students can work on their task lists.

Here are ways to save time organizing individualized task lists for personalized learning time:

- Prepare three different math activities related to the standard currently being taught (essential, application, and complex-thinking layers). These activities may be in the textbook, on a worksheet, or included in a teacher-made activity.

- Prepare three different language-arts activities related to the standard currently being taught (essential, application, and complex-thinking layers). These activities may be in the textbook, on a worksheet, or included in a teacher-made activity.

- Prepare several fun tasks with visual, auditory, and kinesthetic learners in mind. These tasks could involve standards currently being learned or a review of previously taught standards. Allow students to choose one or more of these activities to work on.

- Review the layer of learning that each student needs, and fill in his or her weekly activity list with the appropriate math, language arts, and student-choice activities.

- For students who do not fall into one of the three layers of learning (such as an English-language learner who has not yet learned any English), create a personalized task list on a level that meets that student's specific need.

Personalized Learning Time in Mr. Ong's Classroom

Mr. Ong teaches language arts to fifth-grade students at Lingley Middle School. Students are currently engaged in the following language arts standard:

 The student will compare and contrast the attribute of fiction.

This particular standard is asking that students become proficient in the application layer of learning. Mr. Ong is aware that all students are expected to at least meet the layer of learning that the standard calls for, but some may need to begin at the essential layer to gain proficiency with background knowledge or skills before they move to the application layer of learning.

Making It Work for an English-language learner. Mr. Ong has determined, based on the Student Attribute Chart and a pretest, the layer of learning at which each student will begin (essential, application, or complex thinking). With this knowledge, he provides instruction in the classroom that addresses the learning readiness for each of the three groups. He also creates personalized learning task lists for each of these three groups. He is very aware that with each new standard or goal that he teaches, he must make new determinations regarding the layer of learning in which individual students will begin their learning tasks. For example, an English-language learner named Juanita, who is not proficient in reading comprehension, is extremely capable of comprehending oral information. Therefore, using this standard, if the lesson involves an *oral* comparison of the attributes of fiction and nonfiction, Juanita's personalized learning activities and the oral questions Mr. Ong asks her during instruction would be in the application layer of learning. However, if the tasks required a great deal of reading, then Juanita's task list would have begun in the essential layer of learning.

During personalized learning time, Mr. Ong's students have been given a list of tasks that they must complete during the week; they have 15 minutes each morning to work on those tasks. Some of them, which are structured according to learning layers, relate to the learning standard.

Personalized Learning Time in Mr. Ong's Classroom (continued)

Mr. Ong also includes tasks that relate to previous language arts standards in which certain students need more practice. Because the layers are flexible and customized for each new standard that he teaches, Mr. Ong does not make the mistake of grouping students in a particular layer and leaving them there without good cause while he goes on to teach other standards. Using the attribute charts and some form of pretest, whether it's an observation checklist, formal quiz, or graphic organizer, Mr. Ong moves each student to the appropriate layer of learning.

In grading or scoring the personalized learning time activities, Mr. Ong uses the Personalized Learning Time Task List shown in Table 4-1. He initials the column next to the activity items to indicate that the student has completed the task. He then uses the simple rubric shown in Table 4-2 to determine a score of 1, 2, or 3 that the student has earned for task proficiency and continues to use this rubric week after week so that students become familiar with the criteria. In addition, students use the right-hand column of the task list for each of the tasks that they complete to reflect on their learning.

You will also find a blank form of the Personalized Learning Time Task List, as well as a generic Personalized Learning Rubric, on pages 119–120 in the Tools and Templates section at the end of this chapter. These resources are also available online at www.teachinginfocus.com.

Table 4-1. Sample Personalized Learning Time Task List

TEACHER INITIALS & SCORE			WEEKLY TASKS	STUDENT REFLECTIONS
1	2	3	Language arts: Create a Venn diagram to compare and contrast the attributes of fiction and nonfiction.	
1	2	3	Language arts: Read a newspaper article and answer *who, what, when* questions on handout.	
1	2	3	Language arts: Draw pictures or symbols for each spelling word to help you remember meanings for this week's spelling words.	
1	2	3	Student choice: Write a friendly letter that includes a— · Heading · Salutation · Body · Closing · Signature	
1	2	3	Create a colorful envelope to go with your friendly letter.	
1	2	3	Or share your letter with a partner, and listen to the letter that he or she wrote. How are your two letters similar? How are they different?	
1	2	3	Create a song, poster, or skit to help us remember the parts of a friendly letter.	

Table 4-2. Personalized Learning-Time Rubric for Task List

TASK LIST SCORES	TASK EXPECTATIONS
Completion, Quality, and Demonstration of Learning	3: The student has completed the task to a satisfactory or exemplary degree. The work shows effort and acceptable quality. The task shows that the student gained a high degree of learning and new knowledge pertaining to the academic standard.
	2: The student has completed the task to a minimally satisfactory degree. The work shows effort and acceptable quality. Tasks show that the student gained some new knowledge pertaining to the academic standard.
	1: The student has not completed the task or has completed it to an unsatisfactory degree. The work shows little effort or quality. Tasks show that the student gained little new knowledge pertaining to the academic standard.

Learning the Language of the Standard

The next teaching strategy involves learning the language of the standard. We've already presented some of the research regarding the impact that vocabulary instruction has on student achievement. Learning the language of the standard promotes teaching the *precise* vocabulary that is needed in order for students to be successful with the current standard. Table 4-3 (page 98) shows the vocabulary of four typical standards that must be explicitly taught to students before they have any chance of becoming proficient with the standard's expectation.

As you can see from the italicized words, there is a significant amount of vocabulary preteaching that needs to happen prior to the content lesson. Also notice in the right-hand column that in addition to the language that is embedded in the standard, students need to know certain related vocabulary words, such as *atlas, almanac, dictionary,* and so on, before they can truly comprehend the term *expository text.* During the preteaching phase, the teacher must read between the lines to anticipate additional terms, besides the language of the standard, that students may need to know.

Table 4-3. Vocabulary of Four Typical Standards

STANDARDS/BENCHMARKS	LANGUAGE NEEDED FOR SUCCESS
P.O. 1. Identify the main idea and supporting details in expository text.	1. *Main idea; supporting details; expository text*
P.O. 2. Distinguish fact from opinion in expository text.	1. Fact; opinion; expository text
	2. Examples of expository text, such as *atlas, journal writings, almanac*
P.O. 3. Determine author's main purpose (for example, to inform, to describe, to explain) in writing the expository text.	1. *Main purpose; inform; describe; explain; expository text*
	2. Examples of expository text, such as *atlas, journal writings, almanac, dictionary*
P.O. 4. Locate specific information by using organizational features (for example, table of contents, headings, captions, bold print, glossaries, indices, italics, key words, topic sentences, concluding sentences) of expository text.	1. *Organizational features; table of contents; headings; captions; bold print; glossaries; indices; italics; key words; topic sentences; concluding sentences; expository text*
	2. Examples of expository text, such as *atlas, journal writings, almanac*

Research has determined that the highest student success in learning and retaining the meanings of terms and concepts occurs when the following steps are used during instruction:

- Activate student prior knowledge about a term or concept, or if they have no prior knowledge, create an experience to give them that knowledge.

- Explicitly teach a word or concept definition, and then ask students to create their own definition and visual representation of the word.

- Provide multiple exposures to new terms through a variety of modalities (for example, verbally, visually, and kinesthetically).

- Revisit student-created definitions and visual representations periodically, and allow them to revise, modify, and update their definitions and visuals.

(Marzano, Pickering, & Pollock, 2001)

Children of poverty, English-language learners, culturally diverse students, and students with literacy challenges will especially benefit from a vocabulary preview lesson prior to the actual vocabulary introduction to the whole class. Many students come to school without the necessary background knowledge or experiences that enable them to make connections to new words that are being introduced. It is the teacher's responsibility to provide them with exposure to the language of the standard prior to the actual lesson, so that students can develop insights and background knowledge. During personalized learning time, you might call this group of students to a table where they would spend 10 minutes learning to pronounce the terms, discussing their meaning, and seeing a visual representation of each one.

Concept Attainment

Provide the concept map shown in Figure 4-2 (page 100) to students prior to a lesson or unit, when there are only a few new words to learn. For each term, students complete the four circles.

1. First, ask students to write down what they already know about the term, including any background knowledge or experience they may have regarding it.

2. Next, students read the teacher's definition of the word and discuss how it compares to what they wrote in the first circle.

3. In the third circle, students create their definition, based on their own knowledge, the teacher's definition, and the class discussion about the word.

4. Lastly, a visual reminder, such as a quick sketch or symbol, will help students remember the meaning of the term.

A reproducible form of the concept map can be found in the Tools and Templates section on page 121 at the end of this chapter or at www.teachinginfocus.com.

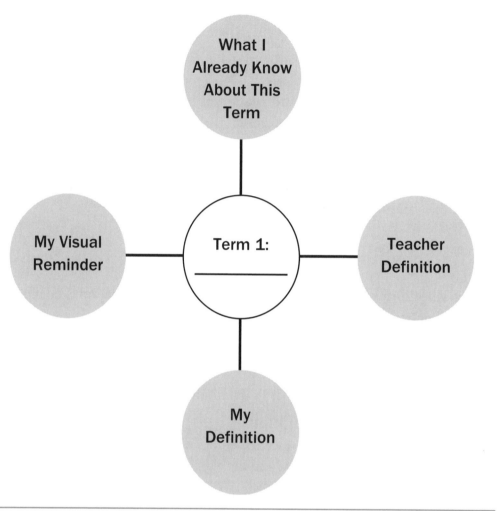

Figure 4–2. Concept Map

Term and Concept Grid

The Term and Concept Grid shown in Figure 4-3 is similar to the concept map but is more conducive to a longer word list.

Student: _____

Date: _____

WORD	CURRENT KNOWLEDGE	TEACHER DEFINITION	MY OWN DEFINITION	MY VISUAL REMINDER
Expository text	I think it's stuff that you read that's not any fun—like information books.	Expository text is nonfiction reading material. The intent of these written works is to inform or explain something to the reading audience.	Expository text is reading material that is true or factual and it explains something to others.	

Figure 4-3. Term and Concept Grid

Scaffolding the Learning

When learning is scaffolded, the teacher initially provides a clear structure and then gradually releases control as students gain proficiency in the new skill. The practice step in the focused instruction map refers to controlled, coached, and independent practice. In a nutshell, that's what scaffolding is all about. We give students a supportive structure. Then, as they gain skills and confidence, we slowly remove the structure, a piece at a time, until they are able to hold the learning independently.

Scaffolding can include any tool in the learning environment that might help a student learn. Scaffolding may be optional, such as use of the library or computer lab. Some teachers may provide the same scaffolding to all students; others may offer customized scaffolding to individual learners.

Characteristics of scaffolding include the following:

- A structure or framework for student learning, such as clear expectations, an outline of goals, the process for reaching them, and the product that will result from the learning

- Step-by-step instructions (initially)

- Students on task

- Gradual relinquishing of control to students in the learning process

- Time-efficient practice opportunities
- Learning that is personalized for students

(McKenzie, 2000)

Specific practices one might see in a classroom where the learning is scaffolded include the following:

- Learning logs, to record and reflect new learning
- Writing frames, to aid in learning new writing formats, such as expository and/or narrative structures
- Math frames or graphic organizers, to aid students in math processes
- Editing of writing (teacher editing, peer editing, and self-evaluation)
- Timelines, to support and guide students with pacing on a project or activity
- Forms, such as student contracts, rubrics, and checklists
- Surveys, before and after the learning
- Concept and thinking maps, used before, during, or after the instruction
- Record-keeping and charting on the part of both teacher and student
- Layers of learning, so that student instruction and practice begin at each student's current readiness level

Plan scaffolding before the lesson ever begins, as you begin to focus on the needs of your students. Looking at the Student Attribute Charts will remind you of each student's specific academic strengths and weaknesses. You may also plan a pretest, which could be as simple as a "3-minute write" in which you introduce the new topic and ask students to write nonstop for 3 minutes, telling anything they know about it. The results help you to make decisions regarding which layer of knowledge each student is ready to learn. Once that is decided, plan how much and what kind of support each student will need and how much time it will take them to learn the new material. In this way, the scaffold begins to take shape.

Joe Jackson's Ninth-Grade Social Studies Class

Joe Jackson teaches at Beaumont High School. Here is the standard that his students will work on over the next 2 weeks of class:

> Compare the characteristics of the New England, Middle, and Southern colonies with respect to the following:
>
> 1. Colonial governments
>
> 2. Geographic influences, resources, and economic systems
>
> 3. Religious beliefs and social patterns

Joe has heard about focused instruction and is currently using the 11 steps in his lessons. He has scaffolded the learning for students, because he knows that initially students need clear direction regarding what they are expected to learn and the process and tools they will use to learn it. During the preinstructional step of focused instruction, Joe created the overall plan for the 2-week unit on the colonies. To determine the learning layer for which each student was ready, he used the Student Attribute Chart and gave a pretest.

On the first day of learning, his instruction included the goals and purpose and brain activators. These two steps created purpose and motivation for students to learn the upcoming content. Joe then created three different rubrics, one for each layer of learning, and passed out a rubric to each student. This ensured that all students would know the expectations for the learning.

On the second day of the colony unit, students became familiar with the language of the standard. In particular, they learned the following terms:

- *Characteristics*
- *Middle colonies*
- *Colonial governments*
- *Resources*
- *Religious beliefs*
- *New England*
- *Southern colonies*
- *Geographical influences*
- *Economic systems*
- *Social patterns*

Joe then passed out a graphic representation frame in which students wrote their current understanding of each term. Then he provided the history book definitions of the terms. Next, after a lively discussion about the words and how they related to what they would be learning, students created their own definitions, along with a graphic representation or symbol to help remember them.

The next three class periods were devoted to the sequential and active instruction steps. Joe provided direct instruction while students used graphic organizers to take notes, ask questions, and create I-wonder statements. The graphic organizers were slightly different from each other, because certain students had some information already filled in for them. Students then met in collaborative groups to discuss their I-wonder statements. They read material with partners and shared the main ideas with the whole class.

Check for Understanding. During the first 5 days of the unit, Joe checked in with all the students to gauge their understanding. Before moving on to the practice step, he wanted to make sure they all had an essential understanding of the terms, concepts, and content of the unit.

Student Practice With Scaffolding.

- **Controlled practice:** Joe passed out an attribute grid to all students with New England, Middle, and Southern colonies listed above three columns. On the left-hand side of the grid, he labeled three rows Colonial Governments, Geography/Resources/Economic, and Religion/Social Patterns. Joe worked with the class to fill in several attributes for each of the colonies using student notes and text materials that they had used during the 3-day instructional step.

Table 4-4. Sample Attribute Grid for Unit or Lesson Content

	NEW ENGLAND	MIDDLE COLONIES	SOUTHERN COLONIES
Colonial Governments			
Geography/Resources/Economic			
Religion/Social Patterns			

- **Coached practice:** After checking to see if students were clear about the attribute grid, Joe put them into dyads to complete it and walked around the room to help. In the last 15 minutes of the class period, he invited a few still struggling students to work with him at a table.

- **Independent practice:** The next day, Joe provided each student with written feedback regarding the attribute grids they had turned in. Students orally shared some of their attribute findings for each of the colonies. Then Joe passed out a Venn diagram with three intersecting circles. He spent a few minutes reviewing with students the process of using a Venn diagram and then told students to use the information on their attribute grids to fill in the diagrams. Joe also worked directly with students who were not quite ready for independent practice.

Not all students will move through the scaffolded steps of controlled, coached, and independent practice at the same rate. Because Joe had checked for understanding throughout the unit, he had a clear idea of the scaffolding that he needed to provide each one.

The last two steps in the focused instruction map are assessment and student reflections. Joe wouldn't progress to these two steps without first providing feedback to students on their Venn diagrams and determining that students had attained the level of learning the standard calls for.

Customizing the Learning Groups

Numerous studies have shown that students who work in collaborative groups tend to learn more than students who work individually. In a 1995 study, for example, Anuradha A. Gokhale researched two questions:

1. Will there be a significant difference in achievement between students learning individually and students learning collaboratively on a test composed of "drill-and-practice" items?

2. Will there be a significant difference in achievement between students learning individually and students learning collaboratively on a test composed of "critical-thinking" items?

After studying 48 undergraduates at Western Illinois University in Macomb, Illinois, Gokhale was able to answer these two questions. Let's first look at the difference in achievement on a drill-and-practice test. The mean of the post-test scores for the participants in the group that studied collaboratively (13.56) was slightly higher than the group that studied individually (11.89). Although the difference between the two scores is not large, we may still conclude that collaborative learning had a positive effect on student learning.

On a test composed of critical-thinking items, the mean of the post-test scores for the participants in the group that studied collaboratively (12.21) was significantly higher than the group that studied individually (8.63). Collaborative learning had a decisive impact on achievement in the area of critical thinking (Gokhale, 1995).

Collaborative learning can be casual or structured, homogeneous or heterogeneous, depending on the needs of students during the learning activity. The key to any group activity involves clearly and explicitly stating expectations—what the group is expected to do, how it is expected to behave, and what it is expected to accomplish by the end of the session. When you first plan collaborative activities in the classroom, it would be wise to role-play the expectations prior to the activity itself. The following are specific examples of collaborative learning with ideas for customization.

Casual Collaborative Learning

Casual collaborative learning is usually impromptu, unplanned, or planned to be casual. It might involve a 10-minute segment of a math lesson in which students gather in groups to study their math facts. Or it might occur in a language arts lesson, where the teacher decides to let students work together on a grammar worksheet so that they can share their thoughts. Or it can be as simple as the teacher making statements like the following:

- "Turn to your partner and state this concept in your own words."

- "Discuss this information with your table and be ready to share an *ah-ha* with the whole class."

- "You and your partner take opposing sides on this issue. Try to convince your partner that your opinion is the correct one."

- "How else could this author have concluded this story effectively? Talk to your table and create a new ending for it."
- "With your partner, discuss the chapter questions on page 33. Then, choose the one question that you feel most confident with, and be ready to share your thoughts orally."

In an effort to be effective and allow for the greatest amount of student proficiency, teachers need to be flexible in their thinking during the lesson that is in progress. If students don't seem to be tuned in to the learning, or don't seem to understand the concept, we need to vary the lesson on the spot. Casual collaborative learning is one method of varying a lesson that doesn't require any planning, just quick thinking.

Mr. Sanata's Class

Mr. Sanata keeps three colored strips of tag board stapled to the board in front of his fifth-grade classroom. He uses these strips during casual collaborative learning to differentiate the learning. In this instance, Mr. Sanata notices, as students are reading their science book orally, that many of them are not focused or involved in the learning. He stops the oral reading and tells students he wants them to answer one question, which they will then share with the group. He walks to the colored strips of tag board and under each strip writes a question pertaining to the content the students have just read. The first question, for the essential knowledge layer of learning, is a *who, what, when, where* question. The next question is an application question, and the third question is a complex-thinking question that involves critical thinking skills. Mr. Sanata then tells each student which color question he or she will be answering. Students have 5 minutes to answer as fully as they can. Next, they get into groups of three so that all three colors are represented in each group. Each student in the group shares his or her question and answer; then each student has a chance to add anything another student may have forgotten.

Structured Collaborative Learning

Formal collaborative learning is a planned component in a lesson. You can customize groups in a variety of ways and for a variety of purposes. They may be heterogeneous or homogeneous; you might group together students from the essential, application, and complex-thinking layers. You might call together and take part in a group that needs help in a specific area, or you might call together a group working on a project to ensure that they have considered all the angles.

Structure is an important key to effectiveness in collaborative learning. Not only do you need to be clear yourself about where you want the lesson to go and how you want students to get there, but you must make the procedures and processes very clear to students as well. Many teachers refuse to use collaborative learning because they say students "get too out of control," or "don't really learn much because they are goofing off." This can certainly happen when students aren't given clear guidelines and expectations for the activity. When first implementing collaborative group strategies, it is important to role-play or model for students what you want the group interaction to "look like." In addition, during the activity the teacher should be walking around the room sharing ideas and thoughts with different groups.

Let's look at some specific structures that support collaborative learning.

Corners. Andrea Lamar is teaching a math lesson about symmetry. The specific standard reads:

Identify the lines of symmetry in a three-dimensional shape.

She shows a picture of a three-dimensional shape to students on the overhead and says, "I'm going to ask you to listen to all of the choices that I'm about to give to you, and then you'll move to one of the four corners of the classroom. Here we go." Andrea highlights two of the lines in the three-dimensional figure.

"If you believe that this is indeed a three-dimensional shape but I have *not* correctly highlighted the lines of symmetry, go to corner one." (She points to a corner in the classroom.)

"If you believe that this is not a three-dimensional shape but that I have correctly highlighted the lines of symmetry, go to that corner." (She points to another corner in the classroom.)

"If you believe that this is not a three-dimensional shape, and that I did not highlight the lines of symmetry, go to that corner." (She points to a third corner.)

"Lastly, if you believe that this is a three-dimensional shape, and that I did correctly highlight the lines of symmetry, please go to that corner." (She points to the last corner in the room.)

After students choose a corner, she asks them to form a circle with other students in their corners and discuss their reasons for being there. Finally, each group takes turns sharing their reasons for the corners that they chose.

The corners exercise can be used in any subject area and provides opportunities for students to think critically: Ask students to make decisions and then to defend and explain them. Keep in mind that Andrea let the students know at the beginning of the lesson that they would be asked to play corners; this sharpens their attention and motivates them to stay focused.

Expert Explainers. Marc McKeon is teaching a social studies lesson about early American explorers. He divides the class into groups of four; each group will become an expert on one explorer. In addition, each member of the group will become an expert in one aspect of the assigned explorer's story.

For example, let's say that Marc has placed students in groups of three. He has strategically grouped them so that each of the groups includes those needing essential, those needing application, and those needing complex-thinking assignment layers. His planning sheet might look like the one in Figure 4-4.

GROUP A	GROUP B
Sue Lin—Essential Enrique—Application Cecilia—Complex thinking	Brian—Essential Linda—Application Omar—Complex thinking
GROUP C	GROUP D
John—Essential Philippi—Application Randy—Complex thinking	Wanda—Essential Juan—Application Brenda—Complex thinking

Figure 4-4. Planning Sheet for Marc McKeon's Class

He asks each group to study one explorer and to become experts regarding the following:

1. Essential learning layer—Geography. For which country did this person explore? Where did he travel, and what route did he take?

2. Application learning layer—Accomplishments. Why did this person explore? What was his motivation? What did he accomplish?

3. Complex-thinking learning layer—Judgments. Make judgments regarding this explorer's effectiveness. Did he accomplish what he set out to do? Was the accomplishment beneficial to many people? How could this explorer have been more effective?

Marc assigns each of the three members of the group one of these activities based on his or her learning readiness. That student becomes an "expert" in his or her own layer-of-learning question and then comes back into the group. The three experts now put all their information together. The final product could be an oral presentation to the class, a project display, or an essay.

Partner Problems. This collaborative activity lends itself very well to customizing the learning in any subject area, particularly math practice problems. Students are partnered and follow these steps:

1. Individually answer the problem or question.

2. Compare answers with the partner.

3. If the answers agree, move on to the next problem or question.

4. If the answers do not agree, review the process that each partner followed (starting by rereading the question or problem carefully).

5. Continue reviewing one another's problems step by step to find the discrepancy.

6. Rework the area of the problem or question where there is a discrepancy.

7. When both partners agree, move on to the next question.

Partner problems can be customized by simply assigning to each partner team-specific problems at the appropriate level of difficulty.

Concept Attainment. Concept attainment involves the determination of certain attributes and the search for those attributes to distinguish between examples and non-examples of a given concept. Students compare and contrast examples that contain the attributes with examples that do not. They then separate them into two groups.

The Ten Steps of Concept Attainment
1. Select the concept and define the attributes.
2. Develop positive and negative examples.
3. Introduce the process to the students.
4. Present the examples and list the non-examples.
5. Ask students to tell under which column the next examples fit.
6. Allow students who are ready to generate their own examples.
7. Develop a concept definition.
8. Give additional examples.
9. Discuss the process with the class.
10. Evaluate.

Students gain an understanding of the concept through the use of illustrations, hands-on examples, and verbal and written ideas with which they are already familiar. Some students will figure out the process before others and will suggest their own examples, while others will still be trying to grasp the concept. Concept attainment is easily customized to meet the needs of all learners, because all thinking abilities can be challenged throughout the activity.

Martin Johnson's Third-Grade Class

Martin Johnson tells his third-grade students they will be playing a game and that their job is to try to guess his concept. He makes two columns on the whiteboard, one labeled Example and the other labeled Non-Example. He has a stack of construction paper with words and phrases that he has prepared prior to the lesson. He holds up the first paper, which says "Hillary Clinton," tells students this is an example of the concept, and tapes it under the Example column. He next holds up another paper that reads "George Washington" and tells students this is another example. He then begins alternating the examples with the non-examples.

Eventually, some students are able to tell Mr. Johnson under which category the words or phrases should be placed. These same students are eventually able to list their own examples and non-examples and tell him where they go. Differentiation is already built into this strategy, because advanced students are challenged, while students who have not yet figured out the concept benefit by hearing other students answer. When Mr. Johnson has run out of examples and non-examples, the whiteboard looks like Figure 4-5.

EXAMPLES	NON-EXAMPLES
✓ Hillary Clinton	✓ House
✓ George Washington	✓ A campfire
✓ A librarian	✓ Snake
✓ An actress	✓ Tree
✓ Zebra	✓ Ostrich
✓ Dog	✓ Worm
✓ Elk	✓ Alligator
✓ Chimpanzee	✓ Snail
✓ A newborn baby	✓ Fish

Figure 4-5. Concept Attainment Exercise

After looking at all of the examples and non-examples and hearing other students' answers, many students believe they understand the concept. Mr. Johnson asks them to look at all of the examples and discuss in their groups what all of the commonalities are. They do the same for the non-examples. Although students may not be able to name the concept yet (mammals), they begin making observations such as, "All the examples have arms and legs," or, "They all have hair or fur."

After this group discussion, they come back together as a whole class to make a final list of all the commonalities from the example category. They also give this concept a name: mammals. Lastly, Mr. Johnson has students take out their journals. He asks students to write a definition of mammals and to create three more examples and three more non-examples on their own. Now that students understand the process of concept attainment, he can use it for higher level concepts, such as democracy, tropical rain forest, amphibians, adjectives, parallelograms, and so on.

Measuring Success

In most cases, teachers will probably do some preassessing prior to the content lesson. This would most likely happen within the first few focused instruction steps (preinstruction, goals and purpose, and brain activators). A multiple-choice quiz can determine what students already know about the content; this will help pinpoint in which layer of learning students need instruction and practice. If the preassessment happens during the brain activator step, the instruction might be as simple as, "Tell me what you already know about . . ." Or, "In your journal, write three things that you know about . . ." The informal preassessment will help determine student prior knowledge and concept understanding.

Once the lesson is complete, the question remains: Was it successful? The true definition of success revolves around how much the student has learned. If you have preassessed your students, this shouldn't be hard to figure out. If you gave a formal quiz, simply give the same quiz again, or give one that assesses the same content in a similar format. If there was an informal pre-assessment, such as a journal entry, ask your students to revisit their journals now to explain their new learning. For example, in their original entry, if they wrote down three things they knew about carnivores, herbivores, and omnivores, they will add on additional ideas in order to show their expanded understanding of the content.

If you have followed the focused instruction map and have taken into consideration the three layers of learning, your lessons will be successful and your students will have gained some proficiency. Success, however, will vary with different learners. It may be helpful to categorize students' successes with a particular lesson or unit to find out how you can better meet their needs. See the student success grid in Figure 4-6 (page 114), in which students have been listed according to learning needs (essential, application, and complex thinking) as well as by uniquenesses (for example, English-language learner, children of poverty, and so on). Next, determine which students have been more successful in learning the lesson standards for a particular lesson. What conclusions can you draw from this? How can this list help you to restructure or modify your own teaching?

Standard: Students will determine author purpose in an expository essay.

B = Beyond proficient
P = Proficient with lesson standard
D = Developing an understanding of lesson standard
N = Needing more instruction

	ESSENTIAL	APPLICATION	COMPLEX THINKING
English-Language Learners			
Sue Lin	D		
Enrique		D	
Juan		D	
Children of Poverty			
Cecilia			D
Brian	N		
Special Education Students			
Linda		N	
Wanda	N		
Gifted and High-Ability Students			
Sean			P
Maria			B
Students With Attention Deficit Hyperactivity Disorder			
John		D	
Regular Education Students			
Phillipi		P	
Randy			P
Omar			P
Brenda		P	

Figure 4-6. Student Success Grid

It's apparent from this grid that regular education and gifted students became proficient in the lesson, while other groups of students, such as ELL, children of poverty, and special education students, did not. A grid such as this can serve as a wake-up call regarding the importance of differentiating the learning or using different teaching strategies during the 11-step focused instruction lesson.

During what steps of the focused instruction map would teachers most effectively use the teaching practices outlined in this chapter? Take a moment to look at the focused instruction map and the list of practices alongside it in Table 4-5. At what points in the sequence might you find yourself using these practices?

Table 4-5. Matching Teaching Practices to the Focused Instruction Map

1. Analyze the standard	Personalized learning time
2. Preinstructional strategies	Learning the language of the standard
3. Goals and purpose	Scaffolding the learning
4. Brain activators	Customizing the learning groups
5. Learn the language of the standard	Concept attainment
6. Sequential and active instruction	
a. Essential knowledge layer	
b. Application layer	
c. Complex-thinking layer	
7. Check for understanding	
8. Student practice with scaffolding	
a. Controlled practice	
b. Coached practice	
c. Independent practice	
9. Teacher feedback	
10. Final student product	
11. Student reflections	

Your answer might look something like Figure 4-7 (page 116).

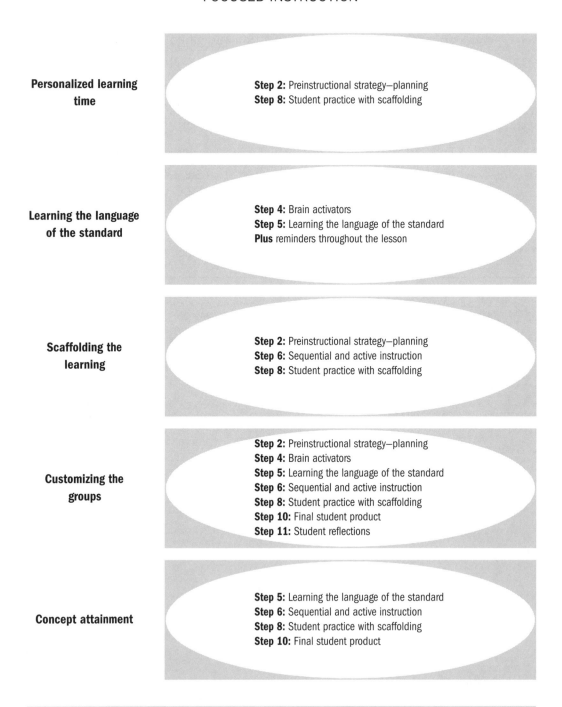

Personalized learning time

Step 2: Preinstructional strategy—planning
Step 8: Student practice with scaffolding

Learning the language of the standard

Step 4: Brain activators
Step 5: Learning the language of the standard
Plus reminders throughout the lesson

Scaffolding the learning

Step 2: Preinstructional strategy—planning
Step 6: Sequential and active instruction
Step 8: Student practice with scaffolding

Customizing the groups

Step 2: Preinstructional strategy—planning
Step 4: Brain activators
Step 5: Learning the language of the standard
Step 6: Sequential and active instruction
Step 8: Student practice with scaffolding
Step 10: Final student product
Step 11: Student reflections

Concept attainment

Step 5: Learning the language of the standard
Step 6: Sequential and active instruction
Step 8: Student practice with scaffolding
Step 10: Final student product

Figure 4-7. How Teaching Practices Match the Focused Instruction Map

Thinking About Your Thinking

Which strategy from chapter 4 was most familiar to you? Which was least familiar? Which strategy most intrigued you?

Between casual and structured collaborative learning activities, which type would you be most comfortable using?

Read All About It!

Creating Personalized Learning Time

There are more ideas for personalized learning time in Carol Ann Tomlinson's *The Differentiated Classroom: Responding to the Needs of All Learners,* under the heading "Agendas," pages 66–68.

An interesting article by Paolo Martin on the need for individualized instruction and student practice called "Struggling Classroom Readers and Individualized Instruction," can be found at the Let's Go Learn website: www.letsgolearn.com.

Learning the Language of the Standard

To read a thought-provoking and inclusive article by Elfrieda Hiebert, Fran Lehr, and Jean Osborn on vocabulary instruction, go to the Pacific Resources for Education and Learning website at www.prel.org/ products.

Bringing Words to Life: Robust Vocabulary Instruction, by Isabel L. Beck, Margaret G. McKeown, and Linda Kucan (2002) provides a research-based framework and practical strategies for vocabulary development with children from the earliest grades through high school.

Scaffolding the Learning

The website http://serc.carleton.edu gives lots of ideas for scaffolded instruction.

Pauline Gibbons and Jim Cummins have written *Scaffolding Language, Scaffolding Learning: Teaching Second Language Learners in the Mainstream Classroom* (2002).

Adrian and Emily M. Rodgers have written *Scaffolding Literacy Instruction: Strategies for K–4 Classrooms* (2004).

Customizing the Learning Groups

An easy-to-read book, *Designing Groupwork: Strategies for the Heterogeneous Classroom* by Elizabeth G. Cohen and John I. Goodlad (1994), has examples and teaching strategies adaptable to any situation.

Learning Together and Alone: Cooperative, Competitive, and Individualistic Learning, by David W. Johnson and Roger T. Johnson (1988) provides guidelines for managing critical issues, such as teaching social skills, assessing competencies and involvement, and resolving conflicts among group members.

Concept Attainment

The website for Instructional Strategies Online at http://olc.spsd.sk.ca/DE/PD/instr.index.html. has an abundance of information on effective teaching practices, including concept attainment.

See also the webpage "Concept Attainment" at www.lovinlearning.org/concept and the article "What Is the Concept?" by Patricia Seybert, at www.accessexcellence.org.

Tools and Templates

The tools and templates in the following section can also be found online at www.teachinginfocus.com.

Tool 11: Personalized Learning Time Task List

The teacher initials each activity when the student has completed it and uses a rubric to determine the score. Students use the right-hand column to reflect on their learning. Teachers should use the same rubric week after week so students become familiar with the criteria.

Student: _____

Date: _____

TEACHER INITIALS AND SCORE	WEEKLY TASKS	STUDENT REFLECTIONS
1 2 3	1)	
1 2 3	2)	
1 2 3	3)	
1 2 3	4)	
1 2 3	5)	
1 2 3	6)	

Tool 12: Personalized Learning-Time Rubric for Task List

TASK LIST SCORES	TASK EXPECTATIONS
Completion, Quality, and Demonstration of Learning	3: The student has completed the task to a satisfactory or exemplary degree. The work shows effort and acceptable quality. The task shows that the student gained a high degree of learning and new knowledge pertaining to the academic standard. 2: The student has completed the task to a minimally satisfactory degree. The work shows effort and acceptable quality. Tasks show that the student gained some new knowledge pertaining to the academic standard. 1: The student has not completed the task or has completed it to an unsatisfactory degree. The work shows little effort or quality. Tasks show that the student gained little new knowledge pertaining to the academic standard.

Focused Instruction • Copyright © 2008 Solution Tree
www.solution-tree.com

Tool 13: Vocabulary and Concepts

This concept map can be used for each new term that students need to know in order to be successful with the language of the standard.

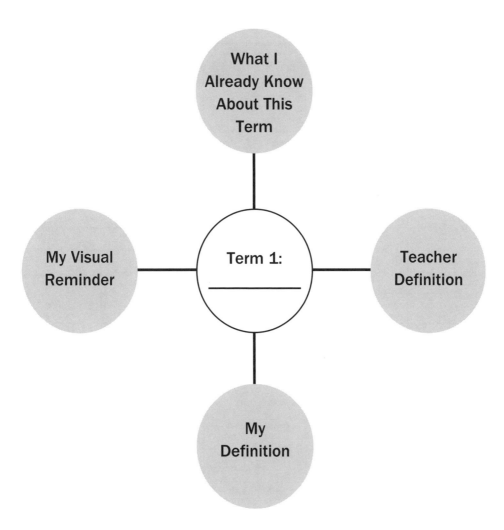

Tool 14: Term and Concept Grid

Student: _____

Date: _____

WORD	CURRENT KNOWLEDGE	TEACHER DEFINITION	MY OWN DEFINITION	MY VISUAL REMINDER

Tool 15: Student Success Grid

Based on a topic currently being taught, group students according to learning needs (essential knowledge, application, and complex thinking) and uniquenesses (for example, English-language learner, children of poverty, and so on). Next, determine which students have been more successful in learning the lesson standards for a particular lesson. What conclusions can you draw from this? How can this list help you to restructure or modify your own teaching?

Standard: _____

B = Beyond proficient
P = Proficient with lesson standard
D = Developing an understanding of lesson standard
N = Needing more instruction

	ESSENTIAL	APPLICATION	COMPLEX THINKING
English-Language Learners			
Children of Poverty			

Tool 15: Student Success Grid (continued)

	ESSENTIAL	APPLICATION	COMPLEX THINKING
Special Education Students			
Gifted and High-Ability Students			
Students With Attention Deficit Hyperactivity Disorder			
Regular Education Students			

Focused Instruction • Copyright © 2008 Solution Tree
www.solution-tree.com

Implementation and Reflections on Your Learning

Learning is not attained by chance. It must be sought for with ardor and attended to with diligence.

—Abigail Adams

In this chapter . . .

- Brain Activator: Putting It All Together
- Complete Sample Lessons From Start to Finish
- Putting It All Together: The Focused Instruction Lesson Frame
- Final Words of Encouragement
- Thinking About Your Thinking
- Read All About It!
- Tools and Templates

Brain Activator: Putting It All Together

This last chapter will take you through two different lessons—one is a two-day lesson, and the other is a weeklong unit. Each of these lessons will take you step by step through the focused instruction model. To activate your knowledge of prior lessons, let's review some of the important concepts that we discussed in chapters 1–4.

Chapter 1 Review

Chapter 1 defined focused instruction as a well-planned, standards-based lesson map that includes the essential teaching components for deep and long-term understanding with regard to individual learning needs. Focused instruction demonstrates that sequential instruction can be engaging, collaborative, self-directed, relevant, and customized for unique learners. To provide you with a visual of focused instruction, we used the analogy of a teacher launching instructional arrows toward the standards-based target. When she couldn't quite hit the target, she moved a little closer or aimed from a slightly different vantage point. When hitting the target became effortless, she backed up to ensure that she was constantly challenged. In the same way, by differentiating the instruction, every student is challenged, yet not overwhelmed, by the standards that are being taught.

You learned that the focused instruction map looks like this:

1. Analyze the standard
2. Preinstructional strategies
3. Goals and purpose
4. Brain activators
5. Learn the language of the standard
6. Sequential and active instruction
    - Essential knowledge layer
    - . Application layer
    - Complex-thinking layer
7. Check for understanding
8. Student practice with scaffolding
    - Controlled practice
    - Coached practice
    - Independent practice
9. Teacher feedback
10. Final student product
11. Student reflections

Chapter 2 Review

Chapter 2 gave specific information regarding a process for analyzing state standards or goals. You are now aware of the importance of determining what your students need to know and to what extent they need to understand it. You also learned how to analyze a standard based on the verbs in the standard. A math example follows:

- **Essential Knowledge:** *Identify* the mode(s) and mean (average) of given data.

- **Application:** *Determine* the mean, median (odd number of data points), mode, range, and extreme values of a given numerical data set.

- **Complex thinking**: *Analyze and solve* problems in contextual situations using the mean, median, mode, and range of a given data set.

Chapter 2 also contained information on the three layers of learning. In a diverse classroom, a teacher makes modifications so that some students will seek a higher level of achievement than the expectations of the standard, while some are seeking essential knowledge because they are not yet ready for the higher levels. The teacher's goal is to bring all students to the level that the standard is asking for, and to bring them there in relation to their readiness level.

Chapter 3 Review

Chapter 3 provided the Student Attribute Chart, an important preinstructional tool. At the beginning of the semester or school year, gather substantial data from formal and informal academic evaluations, as well as data about student temperament, learning styles, interests and preferences, and so on. Then create a Student Attribute Chart for each of your students that can be modified or expanded as needed. This will help determine the appropriate learning layer for each student and forms the basis for creating customized learning groups.

Refer to the Instructional Needs for Diverse Learners Chart in this chapter when planning lessons. This will help with effective teaching strategies that will make sense to diverse learners.

Chapter 4 Review

This chapter discussed specific teaching strategies:

- Creating personalized learning time—Give each student a list of activities at the beginning of the week to work on independently. These activities should reinforce skills and standards that are being taught and that need to be structured for the learning layer in which students are currently grouped. Using the attribute charts and some form of pretest, such as an observation checklist, formal quiz, or graphic organizer, move students to the appropriate layer of learning. In addition to having them work on their individualized task lists, use this time to call together groups that have common needs.

- Learning the language of the standard—Teach students the *precise* vocabulary required to be successful with the current standard being taught. Best practices for teaching vocabulary include the following:

  ▸ Activating students' prior knowledge about a term or concept, or if they have no prior knowledge, creating an experience to give them that knowledge

  ▸ Explicitly teaching a word or concept definition and then having students create their own definition and visual representation of the word

  ▸ Providing multiple exposures to new terms through a variety of modalities (for example, verbally, visually, and kinesthetically)

  ▸ Revisiting learned terms on a regular basis

- Customizing the learning groups—We talked about collaborative learning that can be casual or structured, homogeneous or heterogeneous, depending on the needs of students during the learning activity. The key to any group activity involves communicating clear expectations. The teacher needs to state explicitly what the group is expected to do, how it is expected to behave, and what it is expected to accomplish by the end of the session.

- Scaffolding the learning—Effective scaffolding is a frame that is slowly constructed for students until they can eventually work independently and self-sufficiently in completing the skill. Scaffolding embodies Vygotsky's research on the zone of proximal development, in that it includes challenge, support, and meaningful feedback. Layered learning corresponds with this instructional research. Regardless of the layer of learning that the standard is calling for, teachers can make determinations regarding at which layer each student needs to begin—whether that means backing up to learn the essential knowledge before proceeding to the standard's requirement or advancing past the requirement. Scaffold-building can be initiated at any of the three levels, depending upon student readiness.

- Developing concept attainment—Concept attainment involves distinguishing between examples and non-examples of a given concept. Students gain concept understanding through the use of illustrations, hands-on examples, or verbal/written ideas that are already familiar to them. Students who figure out the process before others do can suggest their own examples.

Now we invite you to read and reflect upon two different lessons: One is a 2-day lesson and the other a weeklong unit. Each of these will take you step by step through the focused instruction model.

Complete Sample Lessons From Start to Finish

Focused Instruction Lesson: Elementary

1. Analyze the Standard

Mr. Ortiz has been working with his second-grade students on using patterns during the writing process. Here is the standard that he will address in today's lesson:

 Use signal words (for example, *first, second, third; 1, 2, 3*) to indicate the order of events or ideas.

He uses a worksheet to ensure that he understands what he needs to teach and to what depth he needs to teach it.

Worksheet for Analyzing a Standard. Choose one of your state standards. Analyze the standard by underlining the verbs. Verbs suggesting more passive activities, such as *know, understand,* or *identify* indicate that the standard is calling for essential knowledge or understanding. Standards that ask students to apply their knowledge have verbs indicating more explicit actions, such as *use, determine, write,* or *read.* The third layer of learning expects students to use complex thinking skills and is associated with verbs suggesting reflection, such as *analyze, synthesize,* and *make judgments.* Try analyzing one of your current standards in order to ensure the following:

- That you are teaching to the expected level of understanding

- That you differentiate the learning to accommodate students' individual needs

Write your chosen standard:

Use signal words (for example, first, second, third; 1, 2, 3) to indicate the order of events or ideas.

What layer of learning is the standard calling for?

Application

Now, think about how you would customize the learning for students of varying readiness levels. All students would be expected to eventually meet the expectations of the grade-level standard, but some would need a jumpstart with a standard that asks for essential knowledge, while others may need a more challenging level of expectation. How would you modify the standard that you listed above for your diverse group of students?

LAYER 1: ESSENTIAL KNOWLEDGE	LAYER 2: APPLICATION	LAYER 3: COMPLEX THINKING
Recognizes signal words (for example, *first, second, third; 1, 2, 3*) to indicate the order of events or ideas	Uses signal words (for example, *first, second, third; 1, 2, 3*) to indicate the order of events or ideas	Uses higher level signal words (for example, *first, next, then*) to indicate the order of events or ideas and then makes judgments about own effectiveness in using these words in a paragraph

Figure 5-1. Modifying the Standard on the Use of Signal Words

A reproducible form of this figure can be found on page 153 in the Tools and Templates section at the end of this chapter.

2. Preinstructional Strategies

Layers of Learning. Mr. Ortiz recognizes that the standard is written at the layer-2 level, application, but some students are not yet ready for that level and others need an additional challenge. He decides that he must revisit the Student Attribute Charts, as well as the prior assignment that involved writing a short paragraph, to get an indication of the layer of learning in which each student needs to be taught. He uses colored chips during the lesson to customize the instruction and practice activities.

Choosing the Teaching Strategies. Next, Mr. Ortiz looks at the Instructional Needs for Diverse Learners Chart to choose teaching strategies appropriate to this lesson. He decides that he will primarily use the strategies of learning the language of the standard and customized learning groups. He will also use the strategies of specific feedback and learning journals.

Preteaching the Language of the Standard. During personalized learning time, Mr. Ortiz calls together a group of students who he feels need preteaching of the terms that will be used in the lesson. All students will receive instruction on these terms when the lesson begins, but Mr. Ortiz wants to build some background knowledge for his English-language learners, children of poverty, and culturally diverse students.

Final Preparation for the Lesson. Mr. Ortiz already has his students sitting in groups of four, but prior to the lesson, he decides what grouping changes he needs to make for this particular lesson. Because he has 28 students and wants groups of four, he will use seven different colors of chips. He also creates a rubric for each learning layer and finds paragraphs to duplicate for certain students.

3. Goals and Purpose

In step three of the focused instruction map, Mr. Ortiz begins his actual lesson. First, he asks all students to completely clear off their desks. When they're ready, he states, "Today we will be using signal words, such as *first, second,* and *third* (he writes these on the whiteboard) and *1, 2,* and *3* (he writes these words underneath them) to indicate the order of events or ideas." Next, he passes out a colored chip to each student. He points to a cluster of four desks and says, "If I gave you a blue chip, please bring your pencil and journal here." He stands next to another group of desks. "If I gave you a red chip, please bring your pencil and journal over here." He continues with this procedure until all students are sitting with their new groups. Mr. Ortiz has strategically placed students into heterogeneous groups so that the essential, application, and complex-thinking layers are represented in each group.

Mr. Ortiz then collects the colored chips and redistributes them. Students in the essential layer are all given green chips, those in the application layer receive red chips, and those in the complex-thinking layer receive blue chips. Students will remain in their heterogeneous groups, but they will now have different expectations for the learning based on their chip color.

4 and 5. Brain Activators and Learn the Language of the Standard

Mr. Ortiz decides to combine the steps of brain activators with learning the language of the standard. He points to the whiteboard and repeats the standard. "We will be using signal words such as *first, second,* and *third* (he points to these words on the whiteboard) and *1, 2,* and *3* (he points to the numbers underneath the written numerals) to indicate the order of events or ideas." Next, he underlines *signal words* and says to students, "Why do you think words such as *first, second,* and *third* would be called signal words?" He asks students to discuss this at their table for a moment. Students share their ideas, and Mr. Ortiz guides them to understand that words such as *first, second,* and *third* signal or alert the reader that there is an order of events in the reading that we need to pay attention to.

6. Sequential and Active Instruction

Since Mr. Ortiz has provided colored chips to students based on their readiness levels, he can use this tool during instruction to customize the learning:

- Essential knowledge layer—green chips

- Application layer—red chips

- Complex-thinking layer—blue chips

Now Mr. Ortiz will verbally model for students how to use signal words correctly. As he talks, he writes these sentences on the whiteboard. "My alarm rang at 6:00 A.M. First, I got out of bed. Second, I took a shower. Third, I ate breakfast." He asks students with green chips (essential layer) to find the signal words and share them with their groups. He creates several more sentences like these, asking students with green chips to find the signal words.

Next, he asks students who have red chips (application layer) to create and orally share with their groups new sentences that have signal words in them. Students with blue chips are asked to serve as the "guide" to determine if the sentences and order of signal words were used correctly and sequentially.

7. Check for Understanding

Throughout the lesson, Mr. Ortiz checks for understanding using various formative assessment formats (for example, oral discussion, oral sentences, paragraph signal words, and journal writings). Because the instructional component of the lesson was auditory, he has a clear idea of student readiness to move into the practice component.

8. Student Practice With Scaffolding

Mr. Ortiz provides each student with a simple rubric to show them the assignment expectations. He has created three different rubrics to reflect the learning expectations of each layer of learning.

Controlled practice. Students are asked to create four sentences together orally. The first sentence will be the topic sentence, similar to Mr. Ortiz's, "My alarm rang at 6:00 A.M." sentence. The next three will use signal words. Mr. Ortiz visits each group to ensure that they are clear about expectations. He provides feedback and guidance to all groups. Students share their four sentences aloud for the class.

Coached practice.

1. Students with green chips are given a paragraph that has been copied from the reading text. They are asked to circle all of the signal words that they can find.

2. Students with red chips are given a paragraph template. The first sentence, a topic sentence, is already written for them. The next three lines have the signal words filled in—*first, second,* and *third.* Red chip students are asked to complete the sentences so that the paragraph makes sense.

3. Students with blue chips work on a four-sentence paragraph using at least three signal words. They are encouraged to use signal words other than those that the class has already talked about (for example, *then, next,* and *finally*). Again, Mr. Ortiz provides feedback and guidance.

Independent Practice. All students use their journals for independent practice. Mr. Ortiz gives green-chip students another paragraph. He asks them to find the signal words and write them in their journals. He asks red-chip students to write a four-sentence paragraph using at least three signal words. He asks blue-chip students to use both sides of a page of their journal book. On the left side, they will write a four-sentence paragraph with at least three signal words. On the right side, they will analyze how well they used the signal words and what other words they could have substituted for those signal words.

9. Teacher Feedback

Mr. Ortiz collects the journal entries, and the following day he provides feedback to all students by calling them together by their colors. He reviews the simple rubric to remind them of the assignment expectations. He will further challenge students who performed above the layer of learning in which they were placed.

10. Final Student Product

After receiving feedback, he asks students to make corrections, additions, or modifications to their paragraphs and then scores their paragraphs according to the rubric criteria.

11. Student Reflections

Mr. Ortiz provides students with the template shown in Figure 5-2.

Dear _____,

Today in Mr. Ortiz's class I learned about signal words. First, I learned

_____.

Secondly, I learned

_____.

Third, I learned

_____.

Students, please take this home and share it with a family member.

Figure 5-2. Template for Student Reflections

Focused Instruction Lesson: Secondary

This next lesson is structured for a seventh-grade classroom with a 50-minute period. The lesson will take 6 days to complete. Elaine Kurtz is teaching a geography unit to her seventh-grade students. Here is the specific standard for which she will create this lesson:

 Analyze how social (for example, family), physical (for example, good climate, farmland, water, minerals), and economic (for example, jobs) resources influence where human populations choose to live.

Prior to Day 1 of the Lesson

1. Analyze the standard. Elaine starts her preinstructional planning by analyzing the standard. She determines that this standard is a layer-3 standard, because students are being asked to not only know and apply information, but to analyze it as well. She knows that many of her students will need to learn the essential and application levels before they can do this. Elaine decides to preassess students through table talks and journals. Based on this information, she will create three layers of learning, shown in Figure 5-3, to meet the needs of all learners.

LAYER 1: ESSENTIAL KNOWLEDGE	LAYER 2: APPLICATION	LAYER 3: COMPLEX THINKING
Understand that social (for example, family) and physical (for example, good climate, farmland, water, minerals) resources influence where human populations choose to live.	*Describe a social (for example, family), physical (for example, good climate, farmland, water, minerals), and economic (for example, jobs) resource and one way it would influence where human populations choose to live.*	*Analyze how social (for example, family), physical (for example, good climate, farmland, water, minerals), and economic (for example, jobs) resources influence where human populations choose to live.*

Figure 5-3. Differentiating a Layer-3 Standard

2. Preinstructional strategies. Elaine uses five preinstructional strategies.

Layers of Learning. She continues her preinstructional planning by thinking about differentiation by content, course of action, and final student products. Elaine creates the following grid.

ESSENTIAL KNOWLEDGE LAYER	APPLICATION LAYER	COMPLEX-THINKING LAYER
Content		
Students will learn the meanings of social and physical resources and will be able to give examples. They will understand that these influence where people choose to live.	Students will be able to describe one social, one physical, and one economic resource, and one way each would influence where people might choose to live.	Students will analyze in depth how social, physical, and economic resources influence where human populations choose to live.
Course of Action		
1) Learn the language of the standard 2) Discussion groups to gain understanding of two concepts (social and physical resources) 3) Graphic organizers to further understand "resources"	1) Learn the language of the standard 2) Discussion groups to gain understanding of three concepts (social, physical, and economic resources) 3) Graphic organizers to show correlation between resources and where people choose to live	1) Learn the language of the standard 2) Discussion groups to gain understanding of three concepts and to discuss specific examples of resources that have drawn or repelled certain populations of people 3) Graphic organizers to show correlation between resources and where people choose to live
Final Student Product		
1) Poster project to show new learning—scored with a rubric for the essential layer of learning 2) 10-question quiz	1) Poster project to show new learning—scored with a rubric for the application layer of learning 2) 10-question quiz	1) Poster project to show new learning—scored with a rubric for the complex-thinking layer of learning 2) 10-question quiz

Figure 5-4. Differentiation by Content, Course of Action, and Final Student Product

Choosing the Teaching Strategies. Elaine will use customized learning groups, graphic organizers, and poster projects. She will also give a short multiple-choice quiz at the end of the mini-unit.

Final Preparations Prior to Instruction. Elaine will create (or find) the graphic organizers needed for the activities in this lesson. She will create three different rubric guides and a multiple-choice quiz.

Rubric Expectations. On the first day of instruction, Elaine passes out a rubric to each student to let them know the expectations for the learning. She has created three different rubric formats and has already determined which students need the essential, which need the application, and which need the complex-thinking rubric expectations. Tool 18, which can be found at the end of this chapter (or at www.teachinginfocus.com) provides a blank template for the rubric Elaine used.

Preteaching the Language of the Standard. When the period begins, Elaine meets with students who have vocabulary challenges, while other students engage in personalized learning time activities. She shares the terms from the standard and shows students illustrations that are examples of social resources, physical resources, and economic resources.

Day 1 of the Lesson

3. Goals and purpose. Elaine writes the objective on the whiteboard:

> *Analyze* how social (for example, family), physical (for example, good climate, farmland, water, minerals), and economic (for example, jobs) resources influence where human populations choose to live.

Even though some of her students are not yet ready for this level of learning, it is the level that the standard is calling for, so eventually all students will be expected to meet it. She then asks students to write this goal in their learning journals. Students are directed to look at the rubric handouts that were given to them during personalized learning time. Elaine gives students an opportunity to read the rubric expectations and checks to make sure that all students understand what is required of them.

4. Brain activators. Next, she asks them to underline the words *social resources, physical resources,* and *economic resources.* She asks students to talk at their tables about what they think each of these words means. While Elaine walks around the room listening to the discussions, she passes out to each student a graphic organizer that he or she will use to learn the language of the standard.

5. Learn the language of the standard. Elaine says, "Now that you've had a few minutes to think about the meaning of social, physical, and economic resources, please fill in the first section on your graphic organizers under the column Current Knowledge." She then gives them her own definitions, which students fill in in the second column. Next, she asks students to open their geography books to the glossary page. They read the definition of the three terms in the glossary. Based on their current knowledge, Elaine's definitions, and the glossary definitions, students now are put into collaborative learning groups to create their *new* definition for each term. They also create their visual reminders of the meaning of each term, as shown in Figure 5-5.

Student: _____

Date: _____

TERM	CURRENT KNOWLEDGE	TEACHER DEFINITION	MY OWN DEFINITION	MY VISUAL REMINDER
Social Resources	I think it means people that like to be around other people.	Valued relationships such as of family and friends	Different people that we care about and hang out with a lot	
Physical Resources	I think it means being in good shape and exercising.	Valued land and air resources such as climate, farm-land, and water	Air, land, minerals, and water that we need to take care of because of pollution	
Economic Resources	My group didn't know this one.	Valued resources related to money and prosperity, such as jobs	Has to do with money, stocks, bonds, jobs, retirement	$

Figure 5-5. Visual Organizers for Standard Vocabulary Words

Day 2 of the Lesson

6. Sequential and active instruction. The class reviews its vocabulary terms from the previous day. Elaine writes Cluster 1, Cluster 2, and Cluster 3 on the whiteboard with student names underneath. She tells students they will be reading from the text and viewing a video clip to gain a deeper understanding of resources and how having or not having them can influence where one chooses to live. Students may choose their own collaborative groups of three but must group with like numbers. For example, if Henry is a #2 based on the whiteboard list, he must find two other #2 students to group with.

Elaine allows 3 minutes for students to quickly form their groups and then walks around the room with strips of paper that have the directions for the assignment.

Cluster 1 Directions (Essential knowledge layer)—Read the geography text on pages 81–85. Use a computer and the DVD to view the video clip about natural resources. Use your learning journals to list more examples of social and physical resources. Answer the question, "Which resources that you listed are the most important ones to you?"

Cluster 2 Directions (Application layer)—Read the geography text on pages 81–85. Use a computer and the DVD to view the video clip about natural resources. Use your learning journals to list more examples of social, physical, and economic resources. Then answer this question: "What kinds of resources from each category would need to be present if you were moving to a new location?"

Cluster 3 Directions (Complex-thinking layer)—Read the geography text on pages 81–85. Use a computer and the DVD to view the video clip about natural resources. Use your learning journals to list more examples of social, physical, and economic resources. Then analyze the kinds of resources that are most valuable to human existence and answer the question: "Why do you think these are the most valuable?" Share reasons for your opinions.

Elaine calls five students from the essential layer back to her table, where she can help them to read the text and work on their journals.

In the last 15 minutes of the class period, Elaine asks the students to go back to their own seats. She tapes a piece of poster paper to the wall and divides it into three sections. She labels the sections Social Resources, Physical Resources, and Economic Resources. She ask students to call out their new examples for each, and as they do so she fills in the chart.

Day 3 of the Lesson

7. Check for understanding—controlled practice. Elaine will combine her check for understanding with the first component of practice—controlled practice. She starts the period by hanging up the list of resources that students called out to her in yesterday's class period. She asks students to talk with their partners (students sitting next to each other) and choose one resource from each category that they couldn't live without. This leads to a discussion about how and why people would choose to move or not to move to certain locations based on the resources.

8. Student practice with scaffolding—coached practice. Elaine gives all three layers of learners their graphic organizers. She explains that students will use them to practice what they know about resources. She holds up the first organizer (essential layer) and explains to students in cluster 1 how to complete the assignment. She gives similar instructions to clusters 2 and 3. Students may work with a partner if they choose to do so. Elaine walks around the room helping students with their organizers. At the end of the period, some students share what they have done and discuss some of the new ideas that they are hearing about resources. Elaine collects the organizers from each student before they leave so that she can determine if they are ready for assessment. See Cluster 1 practice, Cluster 2 practice, and Cluster 3 practice on the following pages.

Cluster 1 Practice. Use your textbook, atlas, or other resources to complete this organizer.

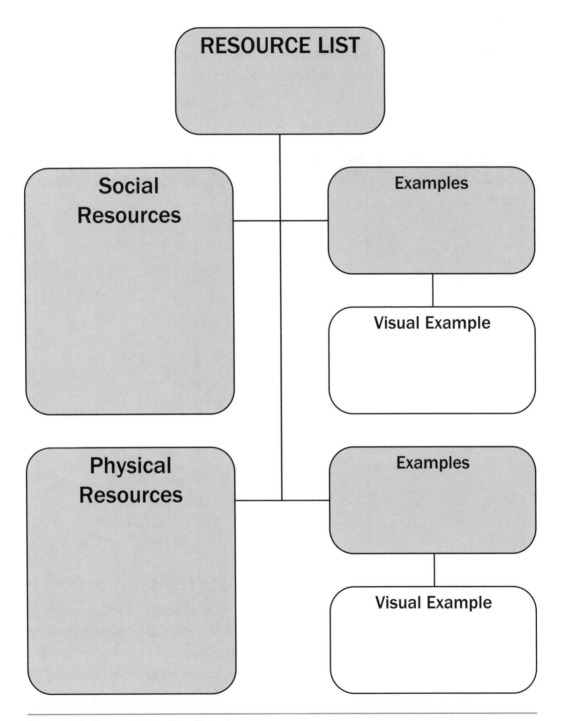

Figure 5-6. Cluster 1 Practice Organizer

Cluster 2 Practice. Use your textbook, atlas, or other resources to complete the organizer in Table 5-1. Give clear examples of each resource, and find information regarding the amount of influence each resource would have on people moving because of it.

Table 5-1. Cluster 2 Practice Organizer

RESOURCES	EXAMPLES	INFLUENCE ON PEOPLE MOVING
Social Resources		
Physical Resources		
Economic Resources		

Cluster 3 Practice. Analyze how social, physical, and economic resources influence where human populations choose to live. Choose a geographical location from a globe or atlas. Determine the social, physical, and economic resources *or lack of important resources* of your chosen location. Which attributes might influence populations of people to be drawn to or repelled from this specific location? Give reasons for your thinking. (See Figure 5-7.)

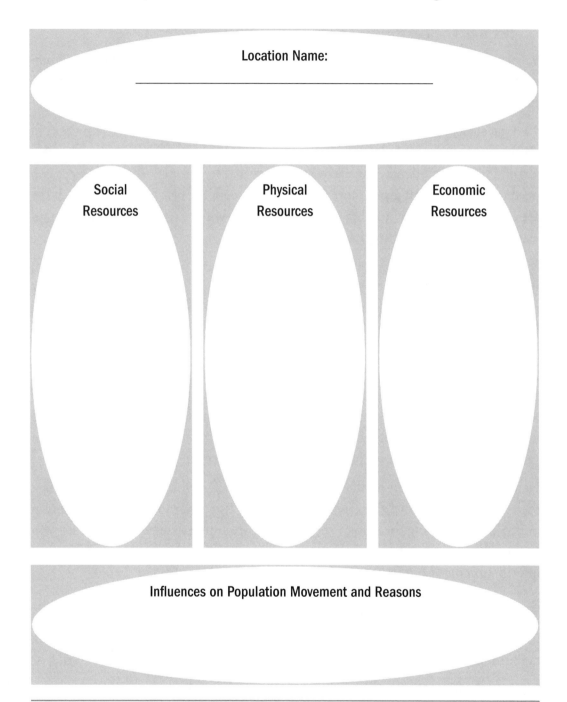

Figure 5-7. Cluster 3 Practice Organizer

Day 4 of the Lesson

9. Teacher feedback. When students enter the room, Elaine hands out the graphic organizers that they worked on the previous day. She has written feedback on sticky notes that she has placed on the organizers.

10. Final student product. Students will use their graphic organizers to help them in creating a final product. They will be making poster projects to demonstrate their learning. Those students who have not achieved the complex-thinking layer will need to be retaught or given more time with this concept before they will reach the expectations of the standard. But for today, they will be assessed in the layer of learning in which they have been working.

Elaine reviews the rubric expectations that each student received when they began this lesson. She asks them to keep the rubric on their desks as they plan their poster project so that they will make sure to include all of the expectations in the project. Students begin planning their project and creating a rough sketch of what the final product will look like.

Day 5 of the Lesson

Students spend the class period using poster paint, markers, glue, magazine and newspaper pictures, and other materials to create their posters. Elaine reminds them again to keep their rubric visible to ensure that they are meeting its expectations.

Elaine has students clean up the room 15 minutes before the end of the period. She then reviews with them some of the test-taking tips regarding a multiple-choice quiz. She is preparing them for a short selected-response assessment that they will take on Monday. For homework, students are to finish their posters and review information on resources for the quiz on Monday.

Day 6 of the Lesson

Elaine has prepared a 10-item multiple-choice assessment for each of the three layers of learning (essential, application, and complex thinking) based on the rubric criteria.

11. Student reflections. Next, students share their posters orally and tell the class the most important or interesting thing they learned about resources. Elaine asks questions of them to encourage more complex thinking about their learning as they share their posters. Posters are hung up in the classroom so they can be referred to as the class builds on this standard.

Putting It All Together: The Focused Instruction Lesson Frame

You've now had many opportunities to see these steps in action. As you review them one last time, envision a standard or unit that you will be teaching. How would you tailor this unit to incorporate the following focused instruction steps?

1. Analyze the Standard

Analyze your standards prior to teaching them to ensure that you are teaching to the expected level of understanding and that you are customizing the learning.

2. Preinstructional Strategies

Integrate focused instruction with diverse learner needs:

- Plan and create various formative assessment activities.
- Choose your teaching strategies.
  - ▸ Who will need preteaching of the language of the standard?
  - ▸ Final preparation for the lesson

3. Goals and Purpose

This is the start of your actual lesson. In a few sentences, what do students need to know, and why do they need to know it?

4. Brain Activators

Tap into student prior knowledge, and create motivation and enthusiasm for the learning.

5. Learn the Language of the Standard

Prior to the content teaching, students need to understand the precise terms of the standard. This will create a common language that the class can "speak."

6. Sequential and Active Instruction

Instruction should always include overt action on the part of the student, such as taking notes, using graphic organizers, discussing the material, role-playing, drawing diagrams, sharing ideas with collaborative groups, and so on.

Essential Knowledge Layer

Prior to the lesson, know which students are in the essential layer of learning in order to meet their needs during the instructional process.

Application Layer

Prior to the lesson, know which students are in the application layer of learning in order to meet their needs during the instructional process.

Complex-Thinking Layer

Prior to the lesson, know which students are in the complex-thinking layer of learning in order to meet their needs during the instructional process.

7. Check for Understanding

Checking for understanding should occur throughout every step of the lesson. This is formative assessment in a nutshell. You may determine understanding through oral discussions, journal entries, listening to collaborative groups as they work, or inviting students to share new learning with questions like, "Tell me what you remember about the steps of the water cycle."

8. Student Practice With Scaffolding

Practice could take place through partner work, problem-solving, a writing journal, and so on. This is different from a final assessment, in that students are not expected to have mastered the concepts yet and will receive immediate feedback on their work. Because we don't want to overwhelm students with a huge amount of content or process all at once, we scaffold the learning. This means that we initially provide full support and then gradually allow students to take control of the learning.

Controlled Practice

Use managed and guided practice with sequential steps.

Coached Practice

Students take some responsibility in the learning with teacher guidance. The teacher still has structures in place, such as templates, graphic organizers, and so on.

Independent Practice

Students should be fairly self-sufficient and may at this point complete an activity without a template, or they may create their own graphic organizers to show their learning.

9. Teacher Feedback

Feedback can happen in small conference groups that include the teacher and several students; or it may be given through written suggestions or one-on-one discussions as students are working on the assignment.

10. Final Student Product

The final student product is a result of ongoing assessment that has taken place throughout the learning. It could include student-written stories or essays, projects, journal reflections, science experiments, oral presentations, skits, and so on. These particular assessment formats can always be graded with a rubric or checklist. This assessment could also include multiple-choice, fill-in-the-blank, and true/false testing formats as long as students are given feedback and opportunities for further learning.

11. Student Reflections

Asking students to express what they have learned or to share their feelings about the newly learned concepts can lead to a much deeper understanding of the content or process that has been taught. Although reflection is often overlooked due to time issues, it is very valuable for teaching students complex thinking. Reflections may happen through journaling, partner discussions, letter writing, group interaction, or class dialogue.

Final Words of Encouragement

The purpose of writing this book with this particular structure was to scaffold the learning for you. We started by providing you with a definition for focused instruction. We answered the questions: "What is it? How does it work? Why does it work?" And we provided a "common language" by listing the important terms that we wanted you to understand as we went through the 11 steps of focused instruction with diverse learners:

1. Analyze the standard

2. Preinstructional strategies

3. Goals and purpose

4. Brain activators

5. Learn the language of the standard

6. Sequential and active instruction

    • Essential knowledge layer

    • Application layer

    • Complex-thinking layer

7. Check for understanding

8. Student practice with scaffolding

    • Controlled practice

    • Coached practice

    • Independent practice

9. Teacher feedback

10. Final student product

11. Student reflections

Next, you were able to answer the question, "What are the standards asking me to teach?" You now know how to analyze the standards to determine the content and process depth to which students are expected to delve.

Integrating the needs of diverse learners came midway through the scaffolding process, and you learned how to differentiate based on the layers of learning that were most appropriate for each student.

You had practice in planning lessons that included the focused instruction steps integrated with diverse learner needs.

Finally, you learned powerful teaching strategies that can easily be used in any focused instruction lesson.

With each lesson you became actively involved through the use of the following:

- Brain activators to tap into your prior knowledge and create a purpose for your learning.

- Thinking About Your Thinking, which gave you opportunities to process new learning and think metacognitively on how you will implement the various components of focused instruction.

- A Read All About It! section with references books, websites, and articles relevant to the focused instruction steps; and a Tools and Templates section that completed each chapter, so that you would have the resources to immediately implement the focused instruction components in your curriculum.

Allow yourself time to digest all the information you have read in this book, but choose the pieces you are willing to implement right away. For instance, if you don't currently do a lot of differentiation, then start with the 11 steps of focused instruction without any customization. When you feel confident about implementing the 11 steps in your lessons, choose *one* of the steps (for example, sequential instruction or student practice) in which you will focus on the layers of learning, and customize that one area.

Positive and effective instructional change results from the teacher who is willing to take one step at a time.

Thinking About Your Thinking

What will be the hardest part of implementing the focused instruction strategies? What would help me to be successful?

How will I incorporate the layers of learning into my teaching? Where will I start?

What questions do I still have about focused instruction with diverse learners?

Read All About It!

Classroom Instruction That Works With English Language Learners, by Jane D. Hill and Kathleen M. Flynn (2006), includes strategies such as homework and practice, summarization and note taking, and the use of nonlinguistic representations.

Carol Ann Tomlinson and Jay McTighe have put together a very powerful instructional model in *Integrating Differentiated Instruction and Understanding by Design* (2006). Understanding by design is predominantly a curriculum design model that focuses on what we teach. Differentiated instruction focuses on whom we teach, where we teach, and how we teach.

Instruction for All Students, by Paula Rutherford (2002), includes chapters on the following:

- Lesson and unit design
- Differentiation of instruction
- 21st-century thinking skills
- Presentation modes
- Active learning assignments
- Assessing with balance
- Products and perspectives
- The learning environment
- Collegial collaboration

You will find an abundance of information and examples of complex thinking teaching strategies at http://coe.jmu.edu/mathvids2/strategies/tms.html.

Tools and Templates

The tools and templates in the following section can also be found online at www.teachinginfocus.com.

Tool 16: Analyzing a Standard

Use this chart to determine the expectations of a standard.

Choose one of your state standards. Analyze the standard by underlining the verbs. Verbs such as *know, understand,* or *identify* indicate that the standard is calling for essential knowledge or understanding. Standards that ask students to apply their knowledge will have more active verbs, such as *use, determine, write,* or *read.* The third layer of learning expects students to use complex-thinking skills and will have verbs such as *analyze, synthesize,* and *make judgments.* Try analyzing one of your current standards in order to 1) ensure that you are teaching to the expected level of understanding, and 2) differentiate the learning.

	Standard:
	_____
	_____
	_____

Now, think about how you would differentiate the learning for students of varying readiness levels. All students would be expected to eventually meet the expectations of the grade-level standard, but some would need a jumpstart with a standard that asks for essential knowledge, while others may need a more challenging level of expectation. How would you modify the standard that you listed above for your diverse group of students?

LAYER 1: ESSENTIAL KNOWLEDGE	LAYER 2: APPLICATION	LAYER 3: COMPLEX THINKING

Tool 17: Integrating Focused Instruction
With Diverse Learner Needs

This chart will help you to determine the needs of each learner and to develop differentiated lessons.

ESSENTIAL KNOWLEDGE LAYER	APPLICATION LAYER	COMPLEX-THINKING LAYER
Content		
Course of Action		
Final Student Product		

Tool 18: Project Rubric

Standard:

_____

_____

_____

CRITERIA	NOVICE	LAYER 1: ESSENTIAL KNOWLEDGE	LAYER 2: APPLICATION	LAYER 3: COMPLEX THINKING

Criteria Customization Hints

In writing your plan for a project assignment, consider the following items in conjunction with the creation of your rubric.

Choose the Teaching Strategies

- Personalized learning time
- Learning the language of the standard
- Customized learning groups
- Concept attainment
- Scaffolding the learning
- Learning journals
- Graphic organizers
- Others

Preteach the Language of the Standard

- Which students will need this?
- How will I preteach the terms?
- When will I preteach the terms?

Final Preparation for the Lesson

- Customize the learning groups for the lesson.
- Create rubrics and/or assessments for each layer of learning.
- Activities/assignments created and reproduced

References and Resources

Adams, G. (1995–96). Project follow through and beyond. *Effective school practices.* Retrieved February 12, 2008, from http://darkwing.uoregon.edu/~adiep/ft/151toc.htm

Alexander, P. A., & Jetton, T. L. (2000). Learning from text: A multidimensional and developmental perspective. In M. L. Kamil, P. B. Mosenthal, P. D. Pearson, & R. Barr (Eds.), *Handbook of reading research* (pp. 285–310). Mahwah, NJ: Lawrence Erlbaum.

Anderson, L., & Krathwohl, D. (2001). *A taxonomy for learning, teaching, and assessing.* New York: Addison Wesley Longman, Inc.

Baker, S. K., Simmons, D. C., & Kameenui, E. J. (1995a). *Characteristics of students with diverse learning and curricular needs.* Eugene, OR: National Center to Improve the Tools of Educators, University of Oregon.

Baker, S. K., Simmons, D. C., & Kameenui, E. J. (1995b). *Vocabulary acquisition: Curricular and instructional implications for diverse learners* (Technical Report No.14). Eugene, OR: National Center to Improve the Tools of Educators, University of Oregon.

Baker, S. K., Simmons, D. C., & Kameenui, E .J. (1995c). *Vocabulary acquisition: Synthesis of the research* (Technical Report No. 13). Eugene, OR: National Center to Improve the Tools of Educators, University of Oregon.

Beck, I., McKeown, M., & Kucan, L. (2002). *Bringing words to life: Robust vocabulary instruction.* New York: Guilford Press.

Bill and Melinda Gates Foundation. (2006). *Teaching all students to high standards in mixed-ability classrooms.* Retrieved September 18, 2007, from www.gatesfoundation.org/nr/downloads/ed/researchevaluation/Diff_instruction_brief.pdf.

Bos, C. S., & Anders, P. L. (1990). Effects of interactive vocabulary instruction on the vocabulary learning and reading comprehension of junior high learning disabled students. *Learning Disability Quarterly, 13,* 31–42.

Boston, C. (2002). *The concept of formative assessment.* ERIC Clearinghouse on Assessment and Evaluation. Retrieved September 18, 2007, from www.vtaide.com/png/ERIC/Formative-Assessment.htm.

Brabham, E., & Villaume, S. (2002). Vocabulary instruction: Concerns and visions. *The Reading Teacher, 56,* 264–71.

Burnette, J. (1999). *Critical behaviors and strategies for teaching culturally diverse students,* #E584. Reston, VA: ERIC Clearinghouse on Disabilities and Gifted Education.

Carr, J., & Harris, D. (2001). *Succeeding with standards: Linking curriculum, assessment, and action planning.* Alexandria, VA: Association for Supervision and Curriculum Development.

Center for Innovations in Education. (2006). *Research-based practices related to differentiated instruction.* Retrieved September 18, 2007, from www.cise.missouri.edu/links/research-different-links.html.

Cohen, E., & Goodlad, J. (1994). *Designing groupwork: Strategies for the heterogeneous classroom.* New York: Teachers College Press.

Daneman, M. (1991). Individual differences in reading skills. In R. Barr, M. L. Kamil, P. Mosenthal, & P. D. Pearson (Eds.), *Handbook of reading research* (pp. 512–538). White Plains, NY: Longman.

Darch, C., Gersten, R., & Taylor, R. (1987). Evaluation of Williamsburg County focused instruction program: Factors leading to success in rural elementary programs. *Research in Rural Education, 4,* 111–118.

Drake, S. (2007). *Creating standards-based integrated curriculum: Aligning curriculum, content, assessment, and instruction.* Thousand Oaks, CA: Corwin Press.

Eggen, P., & Kauchak, D. (2001). *Strategies for teachers: Teaching content and thinking skills.* Needham Heights, MA: Allyn & Bacon.

Gagne, R., & Briggs, L. (1979). *Principles of instructional design* (2nd ed.). New York: Holt, Rinehart, & Winston.

Gersten, R., & Keating, T. (1987). Long-term benefits from direct instruction. *Educational Leadership, 44*(6), 28–29.

Gersten, R., Keating, T., & Becker, W. C. (1988). The continued impact of the direct instruction model: Longitudinal studies of follow-through with students. *Education and Treatment of Children, 11*(4), 318–327.

Gibbons, P. (2002). *Scaffolding language, scaffolding learning: Teaching second language learners in the mainstream classroom.* Portsmouth, NH: Heinemann.

Glasgow, N., McNary, S., & Hicks, C. (2006). *What successful teachers do in diverse classrooms.* Thousand Oaks, CA: Corwin Press.

Gokhale, A. (1995). Collaborative learning enhances critical thinking. *Journal of Technology Education, 7,* 1045–1064.

Good, T., & Grouws, D. (1979). The Missouri Mathematics Effectiveness Project: An experimental study in fourth-grade classrooms. *Journal of Educational Psychology, 71,* 355–362.

Guskey, T., & Marzano, R. (2001). *Natural classroom assessment.* Thousand Oaks, CA: Corwin Press.

Hill, J., & Flynn, K. (2006). *Classroom instruction that works with English language learners.* Alexandria, VA: Association for Supervision and Curriculum Development.

Honig, B. (2001). *Teaching our children to read: The components of an effective, comprehensive reading program.* Thousand Oaks, CA: Corwin Press.

Houghton Mifflin Education Place. Retrieved September 18, 2007, from www.eduplace.com/graphicorganizer.

Hunter, M. (1982). *Mastery teaching.* El Segundo, CA: TIP Publications.

Intel Education, *Teacher and Peer Feedback.* Retrieved February 8, 2008, from www97.intel.com/en/ProjectDesign/InstructionalStrategies/Feedback.

Johnson, D., & Johnson, R. (1998). *Learning together and alone: Cooperative, competitive, and individualistic learning.* Needham Heights, MA: Allyn & Bacon.

Johnson, S., & Kendrick, J. (2005). *Teaching strategies for gifted education.* Waco, TX: Prufrock Press.

Kameenui, E. J., Dixon, D. W., & Carnine, D. "Issues in the design of vocabulary instruction." *The nature of vocabulary acquisition.* Ed. M.G. McKeown & M. E. Curtis. Hillsdale, N.J.: Erlbaum, 1987. 129–145.

Kemp, L., & Hall, A. H. (1992). *Impact of effective teaching research on student achievement and teacher performance: Equity and access implications for quality education.* ERIC Document No. 348 360. Reston, VA: ERIC Clearinghouse on Disabilities and Gifted Education.

Lehr, F., Osborn, J., & Hiebert, E. (2004). *A focus on vocabulary: Researched-based practices in early reading series.* Honolulu, HI: The Regional Educational Laboratory, Pacific Resources for Education and Learning.

Levine, M. (2002). *A mind at a time.* New York: Simon & Schuster.

Lewis, R., & Doorlag, D. (2005). *Teaching special students in general education classrooms.* Upper Saddle River, NJ: Pearson Prentice Hall.

Longert, S., et al. *How to adjust your teaching style to your students' learning style.* Retrieved September 18, 2007, from www.teachnet.org/ntol/howto/adjust.

Marchand-Martella, N., Slocum, T., & Martella, R. (2003). *Introduction to direct instruction.* Needham Heights, MA: Allyn & Bacon.

Martin, J. (1983). *Mastering instruction.* Toronto: Allyn & Bacon.

Martin, P. *Struggling classroom readers and individualized instruction.* Retrieved February 11, 2008, from www.letsgolearn.com.

Marzano, R., Pickering, D., & Pollock, J. (2001). *Classroom instruction that works.* Alexandria, VA: Association for Supervision and Curriculum Development.

McCombs, B., & Whisler, J. (1997). *The learner-centered classroom and school.* San Francisco, CA: Jossey-Bass.

McKenzie, J. (2000). Scaffolding for success. In *From Now On: The Education Technology Journal.* Retrieved February 8, 2008, from http://fno.org/dec99/scaffold.html.

Mercer, N., & Fisher, E. (1992). How do teachers help children to learn? An analysis of teachers' interventions in computer-based activities. *Learning and Instruction, 2,* 339–355.

Meyer, L., Gersten, R., & Gutkin, J. (1983). Focused instruction: A project follow-through success story in an inner-city school. *Elementary School Journal, 84,* 241–252.

Payne, R. (2005). *A framework for understanding poverty.* Highlands, TX: aha! Process, Inc.

Rea, D., & Mercuri, S. (2006). *Research-based strategies for English language learners: How to reach goals and meet standards, K–8.* Portsmouth, NH: Heinemann.

Roberts, J., & Inman T. (2007). *Strategies for differentiating instruction: Best practices for the classroom.* Waco, TX: Prufrock Press.

Rodgers, A., & Rodgers, E. (Eds.). (2004). *Scaffolding literacy instruction: Strategies for K–4 classrooms.* Portsmouth, NH: Heinemann.

Rutherford, P. (2002). *Instruction for all students.* Alexandria, VA: Just ASK.

Slavin, R. E. (1994). *A model of effective instruction.* Baltimore: Center for Research on the Education of Students Placed At Risk, Johns Hopkins University.

Stiggins, R. (2005). *Student-involved assessment for learning.* Upper Saddle River, NJ: Pearson Prentice Hall.

Tomlinson, C. (1995). *How to differentiate instruction in mixed-ability classrooms.* Alexandria, VA: Association for Supervision and Curriculum Development.

Tomlinson, C. (1999). *The differentiated classroom: Responding to the needs of all learners.* Alexandria, VA: Association for Supervision and Curriculum Development.

Tomlinson, C. (2000). Reconcilable differences? Standards-based teaching and differentiation. *Educational Leadership, 58*(1), 6–11. Retrieved September 18, 2007, from www.faculty.rmwc.edu/mentor_grant/Differentiated/differentiated_instruction.htm.

Tomlinson, C., & McTighe, J. (2006). *Integrating differentiated instruction and understanding by design.* Alexandria, VA: Association for Supervision and Curriculum Development.

Vygotsky, L. (1978). *Mind in society.* (Trans. M. Cole, pp. 84–91). Cambridge, MA: Harvard University Press.

Tri-College Consortium New Links for Educators. *About differentiated instruction.* Retrieved September 18, 2007, from www.faculty.rmwc.edu/mentor_grant/Differentiated/differentiated_instruction.htm.

Make the Most of Your Professional Development Investment

Let Solution Tree schedule time for you and your staff with leading practitioners in the areas of:

- **Professional Learning Communities** with Richard DuFour, Robert Eaker, Rebecca DuFour, and associates
- **Effective Schools** with associates of Larry Lezotte
- **Assessment *for* Learning** with Rick Stiggins and associates
- **Crisis Management and Response** with Cheri Lovre
- **Discipline With Dignity** with Richard Curwin and Allen Mendler
- **PASSport to Success** (parental involvement) with Vickie Burt
- **Peacemakers** (violence prevention) with Jeremy Shapiro

Additional presentations are available in the following areas:

- Youth at Risk Issues
- Bullying Prevention/Teasing and Harassment
- Team Building and Collaborative Teams
- Data Collection and Analysis
- Embracing Diversity
- Literacy Development
- Motivating Techniques for Staff and Students

Solution Tree

304 W. Kirkwood Avenue
Bloomington, IN 47404-5131
(812) 336-7700
(800) 733-6786 (toll-free number)
FAX (812) 336-7790
email: info@solution-tree.com
www.solution-tree.com

Ahead of the Curve: The Power of Assessment to Transform Teaching and Learning

Douglas Reeves

Learn the ideas, insights, and proven strategies of the most influential luminaries on assessment in this compelling anthology.

BKF232

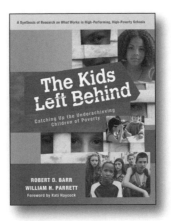

The Kids Left Behind

Robert D. Barr and William H. Parrett

Successfully reach and teach underachieving children of poverty with the help of this comprehensive resource.

BKF216

Total Instructional Alignment: From Standards to Student Success

Lisa Carter

Replace an antiquated education system with a flexible, proactive one that ensures learning for all by focusing on three important domains of the alignment process.

BKF222

Whatever It Takes

Richard DuFour, Rebecca DuFour, Robert Eaker, and Gayle Karhanek

Elementary, middle, and high-school case studies illustrate how professional learning communities respond to students who aren't learning despite their teachers' best efforts.

BKF174

Solution Tree   Visit www.solution-tree.com or call 800.733.6786 to order.